Study Guide to Accompany

BUSINESS LAW AND THE REGULATION OF BUSINESS

Len Young Smith ■ Richard A. Mann ■ Barry S. Roberts

PREPARED BY

RICHARD A. MANN

Professor of Business Law,
The University of North Carolina at Chapel Hill,
Member of the North Carolina Bar

BARRY S. ROBERTS

Associate Professor of Business Law,
The University of North Carolina at Chapel Hill,
Member of the North Carolina and Pennsylvania Bars

WEST PUBLISHING COMPANY
St. Paul New York Los Angeles San Francisco

50 West Kellogg Boulevard
P.O. Box 43526
St. Paul, MN 55164

Printed in the United States of America
ISBN 0-314-81043-9

CONTENTS

PART ONE: THE LEGAL ENVIRONMENT OF BUSINESS

Chapter

1 Introduction to Law 1

2 The Judicial System 7

3 Intentional Torts 14

4 Negligence and Strict Liability 21

PART TWO: CONTRACTS

5 Introduction to Contracts 28

6 Mutual Assent 34

7 Conduct Invalidating Assent 43

8 Consideration 50

9 Illegal Bargains 57

10 Contractual Capacity 63

11 Contracts in Writing 69

12 Rights of Third Parties 78

13 Discharge 85

14 Remedies 92

PART THREE: SALES

15 Introduction to Sales 100

16 Transfer of Title and Risk of Loss 107

17 Performance 116

18 Warranties and Products Liability 124

19 Remedies 131

PART FOUR: COMMERCIAL PAPER

20 Form and Content 139

21 Transfer 146

22 Holder in Due Course 152

23 Liabilities of Parties 159

24 Bank Collections and Deposits 167

PART FIVE: AGENCY AND EMPLOYMENT

25 Agency and Employment Relationship 173

26 Relationship with Third Parties 181

PART SIX: PARTNERSHIPS

27 Nature and Formation 188

28 Rights and Duties 194

29 Dissolution and Termination 201

30 Limited Partnerships 208

PART SEVEN: CORPORATION

31 Nature and Formation 215

32 Financial Structure 222

33 Management Structure 230

PART EIGHT: DEBTOR AND CREDITOR RELATIONS

34 Fundamental Changes 238

35 Secured Transactions and Suretyship 245

36 Bankruptcy 252

PART NINE: REGULATION OF BUSINESS

37 Trade Regulation 261

38 Securities Regulation 268

39 Consumer Protection 275

PART TEN: PROPERTY

40 Personal Property 282

41 Bailments and Documents of Title 288

42 Interests in Real Property 296

43 Transfer and Control of Real Property 305

44 Trusts and Wills 313

45 Insurance 321

Answers to Chapters 1 through 45 329

1

INTRODUCTION TO LAW

Chapter Outline

A. Nature of Law

1. Definition of Law
2. Law and Morals
3. Law and Justice
4. Legal Sanctions

B. Classification of Law

1. Substantive and Procedural Law
2. Public and Private Law
3. Civil and Criminal Law

C. Sources of Law

1. Constitutional Law
2. Judicial Law
    a. Common Law
    b. Equity
    c. Restatements of Law
3. Legislative Law
4. Administrative Law

D. Legal Analysis

Definitions

1. Sanctions

2. Substantive Law

3. Procedural Law

4. Public Law

5. Private Law

6. Civil Law

7. Criminal Law

8. Adversary System

9. Common Law System

10. Civil Law System

11. Stare Decisis

12. Maxim

13. Restatements

14. Administrative Law

15. Legislative Law

True - False

_____ 1. A person may break the law even though his conduct is not immoral.

_____ 2. In a criminal trial, the government must show that the defendant is guilty by a preponderance of the evidence.

_____ 3. A State statute may be valid even though it violates the Federal constitution.

_____ 4. The courts of equity arose to provide relief to those who had no adequate remedy at common law.

_____ 5. Over the past century, the emphasis in a law-making has shifted from judge-made (common) law to legislatively-enacted (statutory) law.

_____ 6. The courts may review the decisions of administrative agencies even though such agencies have their own adjudication procedures.

_____ 7. Because of the many statutes enacted by the legislatures of the States and by the Federal government the American legal system is considered to be a civil law system.

_____ 8. Under the principle of separation of powers, only the courts have the power to promulgate Federal laws.

_____ 9. The most serious crime a person can commit is treason.

_____10. The law is constantly changing in an effort to meet the evolving needs of society.

_____11. In a civil action, the plaintiff must show that the defendant is liable by a preponderance of the evidence.

_____12. The constitutionality of any law is ultimately decided by the President of the United States.

Multiple Choice

_____ 1. A primary function of the legal system is to

a. provide work for judges and lawyers
b. insure that legal rules are enforced
c. insure that no dispute is settled without an unreasonable delay
d. none of the above

_____ 2. A court may enforce the law through the use of such sanctions as

. ines
b. seizure and sale of property
c. imprisonment
d. all of the above

_____ 3. A person who is injured by the wrongful act of another may bring a civil suit to

a. recover money damages
b. have the wrongdoer thrown in jail
c. order the wrongdoer to engage in or desist from certain conduct
d. (a) and (c) but not (b)

_____ 4. While the principle of stare decisis provides that courts will follow their precedents in making subsequent decisions, nevertheless a court may decline to follow its precedents

a. to correct an erroneous decision
b. to choose among conflicting precedents
c. in recognition of the fact that the needs of society change over time
d. all of the above

_____ 5. Which of the following is <u>not</u> a characteristic of a court equity?

a. may provide injunctive relief
b. may reform or rescind a contract
c. trial by jury
d. "clean hands" doctrine

_____ 6. Which of the following is <u>not</u> an administrative agency?

a. Congress of Industrial Organizations
b. National Labor Relations Board
c. Social Security Administration
d. Securities and Exchange Commission

_____ 7. The appeals court decision in the case of State v. Dawson, 282 S.E. 2d 284, may be found at

a. page 282 of volume 284 of the Southeastern Reporter, second series
b. page 284 of volume 282 of the Southeastern Reporter, second series
c. pages 282-284 of volume 2 of the Southeastern Reporter
d. None of the above

_____ 8. In a criminal trial, which of the following is <u>not</u> required?

a. the defendant must testify in his own behalf
b. criminal guilt must be proven beyond a reasonable doubt
c. mens rea
d. a wrongful act

_____ 9. Sources of State law include

a. administrative rules and regulations
b. State constitutions and statutes
c. judicial decisions
d. all of the above

_____10. In the criminal trial of State of West Virginia v. Dawson the party bringing the action was

a. Dawson
b. the State of West Virginia
c. the victim of the crime
d. the Federal government

_____11. The highest source of law in the United States is

a. an executive order of the President
b. an interstate compact
c. the Federal constitution
d. the State constitutions

Short Essay

1. What are the major differences between common law systems and civil law systems?

2. Explain the principle of stare decisis.

3. Explain the purposes of administrative agencies.

4. Why are constitutions such important sources of law?

2

THE JUDICIAL SYSTEM

<u>Chapter Outline</u>

A. The Court System

   1. The Federal Courts
      a. District Court
      b. Courts of Appeals
      c. The Supreme Court
      d. Special Courts
   2. State Courts

B. Jurisdiction

   1. Subject Matter Jurisdiction
      a. Exclusive Federal jurisdiction
      b. Concurrent Federal jurisdiction
      c. Exclusive State jurisdiction
      d. Stare decisis in the dual court system
   2. Jurisdiction Over the Parties
      a. In Personam Jurisdiction
      b. In Rem Jurisdiction
      c. Attachment Jurisdiction
      d. Venue

C. Civil Procedure

   1. The Pleadings
   2. Pretrial Procedure
   3. Trial
   4. Appeal

D. Criminal Suits

E. Arbitration

Definitions

1. Appeal by right

2. Writ of certiorari

3. Subject matter jurisdiction

4. Exclusive jurisdiction

5. Concurrent jurisdiction

6. Diversity of citizenship

7. Removal jurisdiction

8. Pleadings

9. Complaint

10. Summons

11. Statute of limitations

12. Demurrer

13. Answer

14. Denial

15. Counterclaim

16. Reply

17. Judgment on the pleadings

18. Discovery

19. Summary judgment

20. Directed verdict

21. Appellant

22. Appellee

23. Arbitation

24. In Personam

25. Long Arm Statute

26. In Rem

27. Attachment Jurisdiction

28. Venue

True - False

_____ 1. Each State has at least one Federal district court.

_____ 2. The U.S. Supreme Court consists of a panel of three judges.

_____ 3. The United States can be sued in the Claims Court.

_____ 4. State court judges in most States receive lifetime appointments from the Governor.

_____ 5. Federal court judges receive lifetime appointments from the President.

_____ 6. A corporation may be a citizen of more than one state for diversity of citizenship purposes.

_____ 7. A State court may have exclusive jurisdiction to hear a case involving diversity of citizenship.

_____ 8. There is no right to trial by jury in civil cases.

_____ 9. The decision of an arbitrator is final and not subject to review by the courts.

_____ 10. The function of a grand jury is to determine the guilt or innocence of the accused.

_____ 11. A criminal defendant may not be tried twice for the same crime.

Mulitple Choice

_____ 1. To render a binding decision, a court need not have

a. subject matter jurisdiction
b. jurisdiction over the parties to the dispute
c. exclusive jurisdiction
d. venue

_____ 2. The main function of the appellate courts is to

a. keep criminals out of jail
b. review the decisions of the trial courts for prejudicial error
c. hear the testimony of witnesses
d. determine questions of fact

_____ 3. The citizenship of an individual is

a. the State of his birth
b. the State where he is employed
c. the State where he is domiciled
d. any State where he has been domiciled

_____ 4. Diversity of citizenship exists when

a. the plaintiff and defendant are citizens of different states
b. a foreign country brings an action against U.S. citizens
c. U. S. citizens bring an action against citizens of a foreign country
d. all of the above

_____ 5. In a case where the appropriate State and Federal courts have concurrent jurisdiction to hear the matter, the plaintiff may bring the action

a. in the State court only
b. in the Federal court only
c. in the State court or the Federal court
d. none of the above

_____ 6. A party to a civil action who feels that there are no issues of fact to be determined by trial would most likely move for

a. a new trial
b. a summary judgment
c. a directed verdict
d. a judgment notwithstanding the verdict

_____ 7. After a criminal trial in which the defendant has been acquitted, the State may

a. try the defendant for a separate offense
b. try the defendant a second time for the same offense
c. appeal from the acquittal
d. none of the above

_____ 8. The defendant in a criminal trial may

a. be tried without a jury
b. be convicted by a jury of less than 12 jurors
c. appeal his conviction
d. all of the above

_____ 9. In a civil action, proper service of the summons establishes

a. the curt's venue
b. the court's subject matter jurisdiction over the controversy
c. the court's jurisdiction over the person of the defendant
d. all of the above

_____10. In a civil action, the plaintiff is the party more likely to file

a. an answer
b. a reply
c. a counterclaim
d. a demurrer

_____11. Jurisdiction of a court over a party to a lawsuit is

a. in personam
b. in rem
c. attachment
d. venue

Short Essay

1. What is the difference between an appeal by right and an appeal by writ of certiorari?

2. In a civil trial what procedure does the judge use in deciding whether to grant or deny a motion for a directed verdict?

3. In a civil action, what are the essential elements that the plaintiff's complaint must contain to state a claim upon which relief may be granted?

3

INTENTIONAL TORTS

<u>Chapter Outline</u>

A. Intent

1. Injury or Damage to the Person
    a. Battery
    b. Assault
    c. Fale imprisonment
    d. Infliction of emotional distress
    e. Defamation
    f. Invasion of privacy
        1. Appropriation
        2. Intrusion
        3. Public disclosure of private facts
        4. False light
        5. Defenses

2. Interference with Property Rights
    a. Real property
        1. Trespass
        2. Nuisance
    b. Personal property
        1. Trespass
        2. Conversion
3. Interference with Economic Interests
    a. Interference with contractual relations
    b. Disparagement
    c. Fraudulent misrepresentation

A. Defenses to Intentional Torts

1. Consent

    a. Consent to participate in a game
    b. Consent to a criminal act
2. Privilege
    a. Self-defense
    b. Defense of others
    c. Defense of property

Definitions

1. Tort
2. Intent
3. Battery
4. Assault
5. False imprisonment
6. Outrageous conduct
7. Defamation
8. Libel
9. Slander
10. Absolute Privilege
11. Conditional Privilege
12. Constitutional privilege
13. Appropriation
14. Intrusion
15. False light
16. Trespass to real property
17. Nuisance
18. Conversion
19. Trespass to personal property
20. Interference with contractual relations
21. Disparagement
22. Consent

True - False

_____ 1. The purpose of tort law is to punish the wrongdoer.

_____ 2. A person may be assaulted even though he is not afraid for his safety.

_____ 3. A person may be falsely imprisoned even though he is not aware of the confinement.

_____ 4. Appropriation of a person's name or likeness must be unreasonable to constitute an invasion of privacy.

_____ 5. Truth is a complete defense to the tort of unreasonable publication of private facts.

_____ 6. A person may be liable for trespass to real property even though he causes no actual damage to the property.

_____ 7. A person may be liable for trespass to personal property even though he causes no actual damage to the property itself.

_____ 8. Truth is a complete defense to the tort of disparagement.

_____ 9. Infants are not held liable for their intentional torts because they are unable to form the requisite intent.

_____ 10. A person may use deadly force to protect his property.

Multiple Choice

_____ 1. A has committed a battery if he

a. gently taps B on the shoulder to get his attention
b. accidentally steps on B's foot
c. pinches B on the bottom to get her attention
d. (a) and (c) but not (b)

_____ 2. A has committed an assault if he

a. aims an unloaded gun at B and tells her that his to going to shoot her
b. tells B that he is going to shoot her the next time he sees her with C
c. kisses B while she is sleeping
d. all of the above

_____ 3. A is liable for defamation if she

a. tells B that C is an adulteress when C is an adulteress
b. tells D, her husband, that C is an adulteress when C actually is not an adulteress
c. tells E that C is an adulteress when C actually is not an adulteress
d. none of the above

_____ 4. Publication or publicity is <u>not</u> an element of

a. defamation
b. intrusion
c. public disclosure of private facts
d. false light

_____ 5. A is liable for trespass to real property if he

a. unknowingly crosses B's land while jogging
b. plays his stereo so loudly that C, his neighbor, can't sleep at night
c. tosses a gum wrapper and a cigarette butt onto D's front yard
d. (a) and (c) but not (b)

_____ 6. A is liable for interference with contractual relations if she

a. intends to interfere with the performance of another's contract
b. knows that her actions are substantially certain to interfere with the performance of another's contract
c. intends to interfere with another's prospective contractual relation
d. all of the above

_____ 7. A is liable for fraudulent misrepresentation if she

a. induces B to rely justifiably on her false statements of fact
b. induces B to rely justifiably on her false statements of opinion
c. induces B to rely unjustifiably on her false statements of fact
d. induces B to rely unjustifiably on her true statements of fact

_____ 8. A person may defend himself by the use of deadly force

a. anytime he is in his own home
b. if he reasonably believes his property is in danger
c. if he reasonably believes his life is in danger and he has no means of escape
d. (a) and (c) but not (b)

_____ 9. If A attacks B, B is privileged to

a. retaliate
b. defend himself by the use of reasonable force
c. defend himself by the use of whatever force he chooses
d. counterattack

_____10. The tort of conversion

a. includes the intentional destruction of personal property
b. includes the use of personal property in an unauthorized manner
c. entitles the possessor to recover the full value of the converted property
d. all of the above

Short Essay

1. What is the difference between trespass and nuisance?

2. Explain the meaning of "intent" as used in the law of torts.

3. What is the underlying rationale for having such privileges as self-defense and absolute immunity from liability for defamation?

4

NEGLIGENCE AND STRICT LIABILITY

Chapter Outline

I. Negligence

  A. Duty of Care
    1. Reasonable Man Standard
      a. Children
      b. Physical disability
      c. Mental deficiency
      d. Superior skill or knowledge
      e. Emergencies
      f. Violation of statute
    2. Duty of Affirmative Action
    3. Special Duties of Possessors of Land
      a. Duty to trespassers
      b. Duty to licensees
      c. Duty to invitees
    4. Res Ipsa Loquitur
  B. Proximate Cause
    1. Causation in Fact
    2. Limitations upon Causation in Fact
      a. Unforeseeable consequences
      b. Superseding cause
  C. Injury
  D. Defenses
    1. Contributory negligence
    2. Comparative Negligence
    3. Assumption of Risk

II. Strict Liability

  A. Activities Giving Rise to Strict Liability

   1. Abnormally Dangerous Activities
   2. Keeping of Animals
      a. Trespassing animals
      b. Non-trespassing animals
   3. Products liability
B. Defenses
   1. Contributory negligence
   2. Comparative negligence
   3. Assumption of risk

Definitions

1. Negligence
2. Reasonable man
3. Duty of care
4. Proximate cause
5. Negligence *per se*
6. Trespasser
7. Licensee
8. Invitee
9. *Res Ipsa Loquitur*
10. Causation in fact
11. Contributory negligence
12. Last clear chance
13. Comparative negligence
14. Assumption of risk
15. Strict liability
16. Abnormally dangerous activities

True - False

_____ 1. A may be liable for B's injuries even though A exercises reasonable care to prevent B's injuries.

_____ 2. A person is under an affirmative duty to aid another in peril whenever he can do so at no risk to his own safety.

_____ 3. A possessor of land may inflict intentional injury upon a trespasser to eject him upon discovery of his presence on the land.

_____ 4. Negligent conduct is a legal cause of harm if the harm would not have occurred but for the negligent conduct.

_____ 5. A person will be liable for the foreseeable consequences of his negligence even though the actual harm results in an unforeseeable manner.

_____ 6. A person may be liable for negligently inflicting emotional distress even though no bodily harm results from the distress.

_____ 7. A plaintiff who has proved all the required elements of a negligence action may nevertheless be denied recovery.

_____ 8. Whether an activity is considered abnormally dangerous or not usually depends on the circumstances under which the activity is conducted.

_____ 9. The contributory negligence of the plaintiff is a defense to most actions based on strict liability.

_____ 10. A person who knowingly and voluntarily parks his car in a blasting zone has assumed the risk of and may not recover for damage to his car caused by the blasting.

Multiple Choice

_____ 1. The reasonable man standard of care takes into account the defendant's.

a. physical disabilities
b. mental deficiency
c. superior knowledge
d. (a) and (c) but not (b)

_____ 2. The standard of care applicable to a child is that of

a. the reasonable man
b. a reasonable man who is incapable of exercising the judgment of an adult
c. a reasonable person of like age, intelligence, and experience
d. a reasonable person who is mentally deficient

_____ 3. Assume F violates a statute which is intended to protect restaurant patrons from food poisoning by requiring restaurant owners to install special refrigeration equipment. F may be sued under a standard of care based upon this statute if

a. A, a patron, falls down a poorly lit staircase on his way to the salad bar
b. B, a patron, becomes violently ill after eating tainted fruit salad
c. C, a patron, chokes on a chicken bone which was in his fruit salad
d. D, a waitress, dies after eating tainted fruit salad

_____ 4. A is under an affirmative duty to come to the aid of B who is in danger if

a. A is B's best friend
b. A is responsible for B's predicament
c. A is a doctor
d. none of the above

_____ 5. A possessor of land is liable for the injuries to his licensee if he fails to

a. warn her of a known defect which she is unlikely to discover
b. repair a known defect
c. warn her of a known defect which she is likely to discover
d. discover a defect

_____ 6. A plaintiff who sues under Res Ispa loquitur must show that

a. the event which occurred would not normally occur in the absence of negligence
b. other possible causes have been eliminated by the evidence
c. both of the above
d. none of the above

_____ 7. A may be relieved of liability for negligent harm to B if an intervening act

a. occurs after A's negligent conduct
b. is a cause in fact of B's injury
c. is a normal consequence of the situation created by A's negligence
d. (a) and (b) but not (c)

_____ 8. In a state which does <u>not</u> recognize the doctrine of comparative negligence, A may recover from B for injuries proximately caused by B's negligence and A's contributory negligence if

a. B's fault was greater than A's fault
b. B's fault was less than A's fault
c. B had the last clear chance to avoid the injury
d. none of the above

_____ 9. A, the owner of a dog, is strictly liable to B for harm caused by the dog if it

a. digs up B's flower bed
b. bites B when it has never attacked or bitten anyone before
c. bites B when it has bitten someone before
d. bites B when A knows that it frequently chases bicycle riders

_____10. If A's abnormally dangerous activity injures B, B may not recover for her injuries if she

a. assumed the risk of harm
b. was more at fault than A
c. had the last clear chance to avoid the danger
d. was contributorily negligent

Short Essay

1. When may the courts apply a statutory standard of care in determining negligence?

2. What are the elements which a plaintiff must prove in an action for negligence?

3. What is the difference between causation in fact and proximate cause?

5

INTRODUCTION TO CONTRACTS

Chapter Outline

A. Development of the Law of Contracts

   1. Common Law
   2. Uniform Commercial Code
   3. Types of Contracts Outside the Code

B. Definition of Contract

C. Classification of Contracts

   1. Formal and Informal Contracts
   2. Express and Implied Contracts
   3. Unilateral and Bilateral Contracts
   4. Void, Voidable and Unenforceable Contracts
   5. Executed and Executory Contracts

D. Quasi Contracts

E. Essentials of a Contracts

Definitions

1. Sale

2. Goods

3. Contract

4. Formal contract

5. Informal contract

6. Express contract

7. Implied contract

8. Bilateral contract

9. Unilateral contract

10. Void contract

11. Voidable contract

12. Unenforceable contract

13. Executed contract

14. Executory contract

15. Quasi contract

True - False

_____ 1. Contracts are governed primarily by Federal law.

_____ 2. As defined by the Uniform Commercial Code, a sale is a contract involving the transfer of title to goods from seller to buyer for a price.

_____ 3. A contract to provide legal services for a fee is governed by Article 2 of the Universal Commercial Code.

_____ 4. As defined by the Uniform Commercial Code, goods are movable, tangible and intangible personal property.

_____ 5. Where general contract law has not been specifically modified by the Code, the common law of contracts continues to apply.

_____ 6. An informal contract is any contract, whether oral or written, that does not depend upon mere formality for its legal validity.

_____ 7. A contract may be formed orally or by a writing, but it may not be inferred merely from the conduct of the parties.

_____ 8. The courts will presume that the parties intended to form a unilateral contract when it is unclear whether a unilateral or a bilateral contract has been formed.

_____ 9. A voidable contract has no legal effect and is unenforceable by any party to the contract.

_____10. An executory contract is one in which there are one or more unperformed promises by any party to the contract.

_____11. A quasi contract is not a contract, but rater is an obligation imposed regardless of the intention of the parties in order to assure a just and equitable result.

Multiple Choice

_____1. All of the following are relevant to defining the principles of contract law except

a. Federal common law
b. State common law
c. Restatement, Second, Contracts
d. Uniform Commercial Code

_____2. The Uniform Commercial Code defines goods as

a. movable, tangible and intangible personal property
b. movable, tangible personal property
c. immovable or movable tangible personal property
d. immovable tangible personal property

_____3. The Uniform Commercial Code does not apply to

a. a contract to purchase a television set
b. a contract to sell a textbook
c. a contract to purchase a car
d. an employment contract

_____4. A written contract induced by fraud is

a. void at the election of the defrauded party
b. voidable at the election of the defrauded party
c. void at the election of the fraudulent party
d. voidable at the election of the fraudulent party

_____5. An executed contract is one in which

a. all duties under it have been performed by all parties to the contract
b. at least one party has performed all of its duties under the contract
c. there are one or more unperformed promises by any party to the contract
d. the contract is wholly unperformed by one or more of the parties

_____6. Each of the following is an essential element of a binding promise except

a. manifestation of mutual assert
b. consideration
c. capacity of the parties
d. a writing signed by the parties

_____7. A promise or a set of promises for the breach of which the law gives a remedy, or the performance of which the law in some way recognizes as a duty is best described as

a. a promise
b. an agreement
c. a contract
d. none of the above

_____8. A manifestation of the intention to act or refrain from acting in a specified way is best described as

a. a promise
b. an agreement
c. a contract
d. none of the above

_____9. A contract that is neither express nor implied-in-fact, but rather is implied-in-law is called

a. a formal contract
b. an unilateral contract
c. a quasi contract
d. an executed contract

Short Essay

1. Discuss how State common law, the Restatement Second, of Contracts, and Article 2 of the Uniform Commercial Code combine to form the law of contracts.

2. X orally agrees to serve as an accountant for Y in exchange for Y's promise to pay X an annual salary of $15,000. Describe this contract in terms of the following classifications: Formal/informal; express/implied; unilateral/bilateral; void/voidable/unenforcable; executory/executed.

6

MUTUAL ASSENT

Chapter Outline

I. Offer

   A. Essentials of an Offer

      1. Communication
      2. Intent
         a. Invitations seeking offers
         b. Objective standard for intent
      3. Definiteness
         a. Open terms under the Code
         b. Output, requirements and exclusive dealings

   B. Duration of Offers

      1. Lapse of Time
      2. Revocation
         a. Option contracts
         b. Firm offers under the Code
         c. Statutory irrevocability
         d. Irrevocable offers of unilateral contracts
      3. Rejection
      4. Counter-offer
      5. Death or Incompentency
      6. Destruction of Subject Matter
      7. Subsequent Illegality

II. Acceptance of Offer

   A. Definiteness

B. Effective Moment
   1. Authorized Means
   2. Unauthorized Means
   3. Stipulated Provisions in the Offer
   4. Acceptance Following a Prior Rejection
   5. Defective Acceptances

C. Mode of Acceptance
   1. Silence as Acceptance
   2. Contract Formed by Conduct
   3. Auction Sales

Definitions

1. Offer
2. Offeror
3. Offeree
4. Acceptance
5. Objective standard
6. Open terms
7. Output contract
8. Requirements contract
9. Exclusive dealing
10. Revocation
11. Option contract
12. Firm offer
13. Rejection
14. Counter-offer
15. Conditional acceptance
16. Mirror image rule
17. Auction sale

True - False

_____ 1. The person to whom an offer is made is called the offeror.

_____ 2. In order to have the mutual assent requisite to the formation of a contract, the offeror must have communicated the offer and the offeree must have knowledge of the offer.

_____ 3. An offer must be stated or communicated by words and cannot be inferred from conduct.

_____ 4. An offeror's manifestation of intent to enter into a contract is judged by a subjective standard.

_____ 5. The Uniform Commercial Code imposes an obligation of good faith in the performance or enforcement of every contract within its scope.

_____ 6. A contract for the sale of goods may contain an open price term.

_____ 7. If an offer does not state the time within which the offeree may accept, the offer will terminate upon the expiration of a reasonable time.

_____ 8. In order for an offeror's revocation of his offer to be effective, notice of the revocation must be directly communicated to the offeree before acceptance.

_____ 9. A rejection is effective at the moment of its dispatch by the offeree.

_____10. Under the common law "mirror image" rule, an offeree's acceptance will not be effective if it deviates from the exact terms of the offer.

_____11. Under the Uniform Commercial Code, if both parties are merchants, additional terms contained in the offeree's unconditional acceptance will become part of the contract provided they do not materially alter the agreement and are not objected to by either party within a reasonable period of time.

_____12. Under the Restatement of Contracts and the Code, unless language in the offer or circumstances indicate otherwise, an offer shall be construed as inviting acceptance in any reasonable manner.

_____13. When an acceptance is sent following a prior rejection, the first communication sent by the offeree is the effective one.

_____14. Although an offeree is generally under no duty to reply to an offer, by custom, usage, or course of dealing, silence or inaction by the offeree may operate as an acceptance.

_____15. At an auction announced to be "without reserve", the auctioneer is free to withdraw the goods from sale at any time prior to a bid's acceptance.

Multiple Choice

_____ 1. In order for an offer to have legal effect, it must

a. be communicated to the offeree
b. manifest an intent to enter into a contract
c. be sufficiently definite and certain in its terms
d. all of the above

_____ 2. An offer can be effectively communicated to an offeree by

a. a writing only
b. spoken words only
c. a writing or by spoken words only
d. a writing, by spoken words, or by conduct from which a reasonable person could infer a promise

_____ 3. When an offeree's proposal does not constitute an offer because it fails to manifest an intent to enter into a contract, the offeree's purported acceptance constitutes a(n)

a. offer
b. counter-offer
c. contract
d. rejection

_____ 4. Advertisements, circulars, quotation sheets and other similar business communications usually do not constitute offers because

a. they do not contain a promise
b. they leave unexpressed many terms which would be necessary to the making of a contract
c. both a and b
d. none of the above

_____ 5. Whether or not a person's words or conduct constitutes an offer is determined according to

a. the subjective intent of the offeror
b. the subjective intent of the offeree
c. the objective, reasonable person standard
d. none of the above

_____ 6. With respect to agreements for the sale of goods, the Code provides standards by which omitted terms may be ascertained, provided

a. the parties actually agreed upon the open term but negligently failed to include it in the written contract
b. the parties actually discussed the open term but intentially failed to include it in the written contract.
c. the parties intended to enter into a binding contract regardless of whether they actually discussed the open term or not
d. the parties did not intend to enter into a binding contract regardless of whether they actually discussed the open term or not

_____ 7. If an offer does not specify the time within which it is to be accepted the offer will terminate

a. immediately
b. after 24 hours
c. after thirty days
d. after a reasonable period of time

_____ 8. An offeree generally may cancel or revoke his offer at any time prior to its acceptance unless the offer

a. is an option contract
b. is a merchant's firm offer under the Code
c. contemplates a unilateral contract and the offeree has begun the invited performance
d. all of the above

_____ 9. A rejection of an offer by the offeree is effective

a. at the moment that the offeree signs the notice of rejection
b. at the moment that the offeree dispatches the notice of rejection
c. at the moment that the offer receives the notice of rejection
d. none of the above

_____10. Under the Code, if two parties, at least one of whom is not a merchant intend to enter into a binding contract but the offeree in his acceptance includes additional terms for the contract, those terms are construed as

a. mere surplusage and are ignored
b. proposals for addition to the contract
c. terms of the contract provided they do not materially alter the agreement
d. terms of the contract provided they are not material and are not objected to by the offeror within a reasonable time

_____11. Under the Code, if the auctioneer knowingly receives a bid by or on behalf of the seller, and if notice has not been given that the seller reserves the right to bid at the auction sale, then any such bid by or on behalf of the seller gives the bidder to whom the goods are sold a right

a. to avoid the sale
b. to take the goods at the price of the last good faith bid before the sale
c. both a and b
d. none of the above

Short Essay

1. An offer is a definite proposal or undertaking made by one person to another that manifests a willingness to enter into a bargain. Although an offer need not take any particular form to have legal effect, three essentials must be present for it to confer upon the offeree the power to form a contract by accepting the offer. Identify those three essentials and discuss briefly the requirements associated with each.

2. An offer confers upon the offerree a power of acceptance that continues until the offer terminates. Identify and discuss briefly seven ways to which an offer may be terminated other than by acceptance.

3. Compare briefly the traditional and modern theories of definiteness of acceptance of an offer as shown by the common law "mirror image" rule and by the rule of the Uniform Commercial Code.

7

CONDUCT INVALIDATING ASSENT

Chapter Outline

A. Duress

B. Undue Influence

C. Fraud

   1. Fraud in the Execution
   2. Fraud in the Inducement
      a. False Representation
      b. Fact
      c. Materiality
      d. Knowledge of Falsity and Intention to Deceive
      e. Justifiable Reliance

D. Innocent Misrepresentation

E. Mistake

   1. Existence or Identity of Subject Matter
   2. Nature of Subject Matter
   3. Failure to Read Document
   4. Mistake of Law

Definitions

1. Duress

2. Undue influence

3. Fraud in the execution

4. Fraud in the Inducement

5. Innocent misrepresentation

6. Mutual mistake

True - False

_____ 1. Duress in the form of physical force renders the resulting agreement void.

_____ 2. Duress in the form of improper threats must be explicit in order to render the resulting contract voidable.

_____ 3. In deciding whether a threat is sufficient to constitute duress, the fact that the act or threat would not affect a person of average strength and intelligence is determinative.

_____ 4. It has generally been held that contracts induced by threats of criminal prosecution are voidable, regardless of whether the coerced party had committed an unlawful act.

_____ 5. A contract resulting at least in part from one party's unfair influencing of another is void.

_____ 6. Fraud in the inducement consists of a misrepresentation that deceives the defrauded person as to the very nature of the contract being entered into.

_____ 7. Fraud in the inducement will result in the contract being voidable at the election of the defrauded party.

_____ 8. Actionable fraud can usually be based on a statement of opinion as well as a statement of fact.

_____ 9. A misrepresentation of law is usually not grounds for actionable fraud because one is presumed to know the law.

_____ 10. The knowledge of falsity necessary to establish fraud requires a showing that the representor had actual knowledge of the falsity of the representation.

_____ 11. One is not entitled to relief from fraud unless he has justifiably relied upon the misrepresentation to his detriment or injury.

_____ 12. A contract induced by an innocent misrepresentation is actionable provided all of the remaining elements of fraud are present.

_____ 13. Generally, one who assents to a contract is presumed to know of its contents.

Multiple Choice

_____ 1. A contract assented to by a party acting under improper physical coercion is

a. void
b. voidable at the elction of the defrauded party
c. voidable at the election of the defrauding party
d. binding on both parties

_____ 2. In determining whether an improper threat constitutes duress, it must be shown that

a. the threat would have induced a reasonable person to assent to the contract
b. the threat was intended by the coercing party to coerce assent on the part of the person claiming to be victim of duress
c. the threat actually coerced assent on the part of the person claiming to be the victim of duress
d. none of the above

_____ 3. Contracts assented to under each of the following conditions are voidable at the election of the innocent party except

a. duress resulting from improper threats
b. undue influence
c. fraud in the execution
d. fraud in the inducement

_____ 4. The requisite elements of fraud in the inducement include

a. a false representation of material fact.
b. a representation made with knowledge of its falsity and the intention to deceive
c. a false representation justifiably relied upon
d. all of the elements above are required to be shown

_____ 5. Silence may constitute a false representation actionable as fraud in all of the following instances except

a. where one party's prior representation was innocently made but later discovered to be false before the making of the contract
b. where a fiduciary relationship exists between the parties
c. where two parties are engaged in an arm's length business transaction characterized by good faith and commercial reasonableness
d. Where one party is actively concealing a fact material to the transaction

_____ 6. Knowledge of falsity and intention to deceive under fraud in the inducement may be shown by

a. actual knowledge of its falsity
b. lack of belief of the statement's truthfulness
c. reckless indifference as to its truthfulness
d. all of the above

_____ 7. In general, the question of "mistake" in the formation of a contract is judged according to

a, the subjective understanding of the mistaken party only
b. the subjective understanding of the innocent party only
c. the subjective understanding of both parties
d. on objective, reasonable person standard

_____ 8. The law grants relief in a situation involving mistake only where there has been

a. a unilateral mistake by one party as to the nature of the subject matter of the contract
b. a mutual mistake of material fact
c. a unilateral mistake by one party to the contract occasioned by his failure to read the document before assenting to it
d. a unilateral mistake by one party to the contract as to its legal effect

_____ 9. In order for an act or threat to constitute duress, it needs to be at least

a. contrary to public policy
b. tortious but not necessarily criminal
c. a criminal act or threat
d. none of the above

_____10. Contracts entered into by persons in the following relationships would be scrutinized carefully for undue influence except that between

a. husband and wife
b. factory owner and supplier
c. trustee and beneficiary
d. principal and agent

Short Essay

1. Identify the types of duress and discuss the legal effect of each.

2. Identify the types of fraud, their legal effect on the agreement, and the elements that must be shown to establish the existence of each.

3. X and Y enter into a contract under which X agreed to ship its newspaper, the <u>Morning Disturber</u>, to Y, a distributer of newspapers in Smalltown, U.S.A. In order to sell a morning newspaper, Y must receive the papers and have them on the newstand by 12 noon. Accordingly, the parties agreed to ship the papers from X's plant in Bigtown, U.S.A., to Smalltown on the "Silver Streak", a train that arrives in Smalltown at 10:00 a.m. Unbeknownst to either party, however, the "Silver Streak's" schedule was to be changed effective the first date of their contract so that it will not arrive in Smalltown until 2 p.m. No other trains pass through Smalltown and shipment of the newspapers by truch or by airplane is impracticable. Y sues X for breach of contract when the first shipment of papers arrives too late for him to sell. What result?

8

CONSIDERATION

<u>Chapter Outline</u>

A. Legal Sufficiency

1. Definition
2. Unilateral Contracts
3. Bilateral Contracts
4. Adequacy
5. Mutuality of Obligation
   a. Illusory Promises
   b. Output and Requirements Contracts
   c. Exclusive Dealing Contracts
   d. Conditional Contracts
6. Pre-existing Public Obligation
7. Pre-existing Contractual Obligation
   a. Modification of a Pre-existing Contract
   b. Settlement of an Undisputed Debt
   c. Settlement of a Disputed Debt
   d. Substituted Contracts Distinguished

B. Bargained-For Exchange

1. Past Consideration
2. Moral Obligation
3. Third Parties

C. Contracts Without Consideration

1. Promise to Pay Debt Barred by the Statute of Limitations
2. Promise to Pay Debt Discharged in Bankruptcy
3. Promissory Estoppel
4. Contracts Under Seal
5. Other Promises Which Require No Consideration
    a. Renunciation
    b. Firm Offer

Definitions

1. Consideration

2. Legal detriment

3. Legal benefit

4. Illusory promise

5. Undisputed debt

6. Disputed debt

7. Substituted contract

8. Past consideration

9. Promissory estoppel

10. Firm offer

True - False

_____ 1. The doctrine of consideration requires only that the promise or performance of one party be legally sufficient.

_____ 2. To be legally sufficient, the consideration for the promise must be either a legal detriment to the promisor or a legal benefit to the promisee.

_____ 3. The adequacy of consideration is crucial to the issue of legal sufficiency.

_____ 4. A contract under which the parties' obligation to perform arises only on the happening of a stated event lacks the requisite mutuality of obligation if the specified event may never occur.

_____ 5. The performance of a pre-existing contractual obligation that is neither doubtful nor the subject of honest dispute is not legally sufficient consideration.

_____ 6. At common law, a modification of an existing contract does not need to be supported by some new consideration.

_____ 7. The payment of a sum of money in consideration of a promise to discharge a matured undisputed debt for services rendered in an amount larger than the sum paid is legally sufficient consideration to support the promise of discharge.

_____ 8. The bargained-for exchange element of consideration is not satisfied when a promise is given to satisfy a pre-existing moral obligation.

_____ 9. Consideration to support a promise may be given to a third person other than the promisor provided the promisor bargains for that exchange.

_____ 10. In the absence of legal consideration, a promise may nevertheless be enforceable under the doctrine of promissory estoppel even if the promisee has not relied on the promise to his detriment.

_____ 11. Under the Code, a merchant's firm offer to buy or sell goods is not revocable for lack of consideration, during the time stated that it is open or if no time is stated, for a reasonable time, but in either event for a period not to exceed three months.

Multiple Choice

_____ 1. The requirement of consideration is satisfied by

a. a promise exchanged for a promise
b. a promise exchanged for an act
c. a promise exchanged for a forbearance to act
d. all of the above

_____ 2. To be leaglly sufficient, the consideration for a promise must be

a. a legal detriment to the promisee
b. a legal benefit to the promisor
c. either a legal detriment to the promisee or a legal benefit to the promisor
d. both a legal detriment to the promisee and a legal benefit to the promisor

_____ 3. A contract in which a promise is exchanged for an act or a forbearance to act is called

a. a unilateral contract
b. a bilateral contract
c. a gratuitous contract
d. none of the above

_____ 4. A promise to purchase such goods as the promisor may "desire" or "wish" to buy is called

a. an exclusive dealing contract
b. an illusory promise
c. an output contract
d. a requirements contract

_____ 5. Which of the following is legally sufficient consideration?

a. the performance of a pre-existing public obligation
b. the performance of a pre-existing contractual obligation
c. the settlement of an undisputed matured debt of $10,000 arising out of the purchase of land for $8,500
d. the settlement of a debt subject to honest dispute as to its amount

_____ 6. A promise made on account of something that the promisee has already done is called

a. a moral obligation
b. past consideration
c. an illusory promise
d. substituted contract

_____ 7. Which of the following operates as a sufficient promise by a debtor to pay a debt barred by the statute of limitations

a. a voluntary, unqualified admission that the debt was owing
b. a partial payment of the debt
c. a statement that the statute of limitations will not be pleaded as a defense
d. all of the above

_____ 8. Which of the following is not a requirement under the Bankruptcy Reform Act of 1978 for a promise to pay a debt discharged in bankruptcy to be enforced?

a. the debtor's promise must be made before the discharge of the debt is granted
b. the debtor's promise must be in writing
c. the debtor does not revoke the promise within thirty days after the promise becomes enforceable
d. the debtor, if an individual, must be informed of his legal right and the effects of his new promise by the bankruptcy court

_____ 9. A promise made under circumstances that should lead the promisor reasonably to expect that the promisee will be induced by the promise to act or forbear from acting in reliance on the promise may be enforceable under the doctrine of

a. gratuitous promises
b. promissory estoppel
c. waiver
d. res ipsa loquitur

_____10. Under the Code, which of the following promises requires consideration to be binding?

a. a promise under seal
b. a written and signed renunciation of a right arising out of a contractual breach
c. a good faith modification of an existing contract
d. a merchant's firm offer

Short Essay

1. Discuss briefly what is meant by "mutuality of consideration". Define the terms "legal detriment" and "legal benefit".

2. What are the essential elements of consideration? Is the adequacy of consideration a concern in determining legal sufficiency? Explain.

3. Are illusory promises enforceable? Why? How do output and requirements contracts differ from illusory promises?

9

ILLEGAL BARGAINS

Chapter Outline

A. Violations of Statutes

1. Licensing Statutes
2. Gambling Statutes
3. Sunday Statutes
4. Usury Statutes

B. Violations of Public Policy

1. Tortious Conduct
2. Common Law Restraints of Trade
   a. Sale of a Business
   b. Employment Contracts
3. Obstructing the Administration of Justice
4. Corrupting Public Officials
5. Exculpatory Clauses
6. Unconscionable Contracts

C. Effect of Illegality

1. Unenforceability
2. Exceptions
   a. Party Withdrawing Before Performance
   b. Party Protected by Statute
   c. Party Not Equally at Fault
   d. Party Ignorant to Facts Making Bargain Illegal
   e. Partial Illegality

Definitions

1. Licensing statute

2. "Blue Laws"

3. Usury statute

4. Exculpatory clause

5. Unconscionable contracts

True - False

_____ 1. Legality of objective is one of the essential requirements of a binding promise or agreement.

_____ 2. In the absence of a specific statutory provision, an unlicensed person engaged in a business or profession for which a license is required cannot recover for services rendered if the licensing statute was enacted in order to raise revenue.

_____ 3. A regulatory licensing statute is one designed to protect the public against unqualified persons.

_____ 4. Some states have enacted "Blue Laws" that adopt the common law rule that a valid contract may not be entered into on Sunday.

_____ 5. Usury statutes establish the minimum rate of permissible interest that may be contracted for between a lender and a borrower of money.

_____ 6. An exculpatory clause is a contractual clause that exempts a party from liability for his own poor business judgment in entering into a contract.

_____ 7. If a court finds that a part of a contract is unconscionable, it must deny enforcement of the entire contract.

_____ 8. Ordinarily the entire agreement is unenforceable if any part of it is illegal.

_____ 9. Subject to a few exceptions, neither party to an illegal contract can sue the other for breach nor recover for any performance rendered.

Multiple Choice

_____ 1. An agreement is illegal and unenforceable if its formation or performance is

a. criminal
b. tortious
c. contrary to public policy
d. all of the above

_____ 2. A regulatory licensing statute is one intended to

a. raise revenue
b. protect the public against unqualified persons
c. prevent gambling
d. prevent certain types of commercial activity on Sunday

_____ 3. A statute that establishes a maximum rate of permissible interest that might be contracted for between a lender and a borrower of money is called

a. a usury statute
b. a "Blue Law"
c. a "Blue Sky" law
d. a "savings and loan" law

_____ 4. At the current time, an agreement not to compete with one's employer during one's employment is enforceable if

a. the purpose of the restraint is to protect the employer's business
b. the restraint is no more extensive than is reasonably necessary to protect the employer's business
c. both (a) and (b)
d. neither (a) nor (b)

_____ 5. An agreement in a contract that attempts to excuse one party from liability for her own negligence is called

a. a clause obstructing the administration of justice
b. an exculpatory clause
c. a restraint of trade
d. an illusory promise

_____ 6. A state statute that prohibits the sale of unregistered securities is called

a. a "Blue Law"
b. a "Blue Sky Law"
c. a restraint of trade
d. an usury statute

_____ 7. In considering whether a convenant not to compete included in the sale of a business is reasonable, courts will consider all of the following factors except

a. the geographic area covered
b. the time period for which the restraint is to be in effect
c. the activities that the restraint prohibits the promisor from engaging in
d. the price that the promisee paid for the business

_____ 8. In general, if a promise is illegal

a. only the promisor can sue the promisee for breach and recover any performance rendered
b. only the promisee can sue the promisor for breach and recover any performance rendered
c. neither the promisor nor the promisee can sue the other for breach and recover any performance rendered
d. both the promisor and the promisee can sue the other for breach and recover any performance rendered

_____ 9. All of the following situations represent exceptions to the strict rule of unenforceability of illegal agreements except

a. where a party to the illegal agreement withdraws from the transaction prior to performance
b. where one of the parties to the agreement is a party protected by the statute violated
c. where the parties are not equally at fault
d. where the parties are in pari dilecto

Short Essay

1. Why are illegal agreements not called contracts?
   Why are they rendered unenforceable?

2. What are the two types of licensing statutes?
   How do they differ in their legal effect if violated?

10

CONTRACTUAL CAPACITY

<u>Chapter Outline</u>

A. Minors

  1. Liability for Necessaries
  2. Liability on Contracts
     a. Ratification
     b. Disaffirmance
  3. Liability for Misrepresentation of Age
  4. Liability for Tort Connected with Contract

B. Incompetent Persons
  1. Mental Illness or Defect
  2. Person Under Guardianship

C. Intoxicated Persons

Definitions

1. Contractual capacity

2. Minor

3. Necessaries

4. Ratification

5. Disaffirmance

6. Guradianship

True - False

_____ 1. As a general rule, a contract entered into by a minor is void and without legal effect.

_____ 2. Recovery for necessaries furnished to a minor is based upon the reasonable value of the item furnished and not the contract price.

_____ 3. A ratification of a contract must be express in order to be effective.

_____ 4. A minor cannot ratify a contract until he has attained his majority.

_____ 5. Except in the case of a contract to transfer land, a minor can disaffirm a contract before attaining his majority or within a reasonable time thereafter.

_____ 6. A disaffirmance must be express and cannot be implied from the conduct.

_____ 7. Under the Code, a person buying goods from a minor has the power to transfer valid title to the goods to a good faith purchaser for value.

_____ 8. In most States, a minor who fraudulently misrepresented his age at the time the contract was entered into may nevertheless disaffirm the contract.

_____ 9. If a tort and a contract are so connected that to enforce the tort action the court must enforce the minor's contract, the court will enforce the contract and the minor will be liable in tort.

_____10. In order to prove that a person with a mental defect lacks the necessary capacity to enter into a contract, it must be shown that the person is permanently insane.

_____11. If property of an individual is under guardianship by court order, contracts entered into by that individual are voidable at his election.

_____12. As is the case with minors and incompetents, intoxicated persons are liable in quasi-contract for necessaries furnished during their incapacity.

Multiple Choice

_____ 1. A person lacks contractual capacity if she is

a. a minor
b. incompetent
c. intoxicated
d. all of the above

_____ 2. In nearly all jurisdictions today, the age limit of minority has been set by statute at

a. sixteen years of age
b. eighteen years of age
c. twenty-one years of age
d. twenty-five years of age

_____ 3. Except for a contract for necessaries, a contract entered into by a minor is

a. voidable at the election of the minor
b. voidable at the election of the other party
c. void and without legal effect
d. illegal and unenforceable

_____ 4. In a contract for necessaries, a minor is liable for

a. the list price of the items furnished
b. the agreed price of the items furnished
c. the reasonable value of the items furnished
d. the wholesale cost of the items furnished

_____ 5. If a minor purchases a car and then continues to use it for one year after obtaining his majority his action constitutes

a. a disaffirmance of the contract
b. a ratification of the contract
c. a breach of the contract
d. none of the above

_____ 6. A minor may disaffirm a contract for personal property

a. before attaining majority
b. on the day he attains majority
c. within a reasonable time after reaching majority
d. all of the above

_____ 7. A person who lacks sufficient mental capacity to enter into a contract is one who is

a. adjudicated incompetent by a court decree
b. incompetent, although not adjucated as such by a court decree
c. unable to understand the nature and effect of his act
d. all of the above

_____ 8. One does not possess sufficient contractual capacity to enter into a contract if it is shown that he is

a. slightly intoxicated
b. unable to understand the nature and consequences of his acts
c. intoxication never deprives one of contractual capacity
d. none of the above

_____ 9. Which of the following is (are) liable in quasi-contract for necessaries furnished to them during their incapacity?

a. emancipated minors
b. persons incompetent but not so adjudicated
c. intoxicated persons
d. all of the above

Short Essay

1. Define what is meant by the word "necessaries" and state what types of items are "necessaries".

2. How does a person's duty on disaffirmance differ if her lack of contractual capacity is a result of her minority, incompetency, and intoxication?

11

CONTRACTS IN WRITING

Chapter Outline

I. Statute of Frauds

   A. Contracts Within the Statute of Frauds
      1. Executor - Administrator Provisions
      2. Suretyship Provision
         a. Promise must be collateral
         b. Main purpose doctrine
         c. Promise made to debtor
      3. Marriage Provision
      4. Land Contract Provision
      5. One Year Provision
         a. The possibility test
         b. Computation of time
         c. Full performance by one party
      6. Sale of Goods
      7. Other U.C.C. Statute of Frauds Provisions
         a. Sale of securities
         b. Security interest in personal property
         c. Sales of other kinds of personal property
      8. Modification of Rescission of Contracts Within the Statute of Frauds
   B. Methods of Compliance
      1. A Writing or Memorandum
         a. General contract provisions
         b. U.C.C. provisions
      2. Other Methods of Compliance Under the U.C.C.
         a. Written confirmation
         b. Admission
         c. Specially manufactured goods
         d. Delivery of payment and acceptance of goods

C. Effect of Noncompliance

II. Parol Evidence Rule

A. The Rule
B. Situations to Which the Rule Does Not Apply
C. Supplemental Evidence

III. Interpretation of Contracts

Definitions

1. Surety

2. Collateral promise

3. Main purpose doctrine

4. Parol evidence

5. Course of dealing

6. Usage of trade

7. Course of performance

True - False

_____ 1. A contract "within" the Statute of Frauds need not comply with the requirements of the Statute to be enforceable.

_____ 2. If an executor or administrator promises to answer personally for the duty of the decedent, the promise is unenforceable unless in writing.

_____ 3. A promise to a creditor to perform the duties and obligations of a third party is "collateral" and therefore subject to the Statute of Frauds when the promise is to pay only upon the default of the one primarily obligated.

_____ 4. An oral promise made to a debtor to pay his debt to a third party is not enforceable.

_____ 5. All contracts not to be performed within one year of when performance is to begin must be in writing.

_____ 6. The Uniform Commercial Code provides that a contract for the sale of goods for the price of $5,000 or more is not enforceable unless it satisfies the requirements of the Statute of Frauds.

_____ 7. In order to comply with the requirements of most Statutes of Frauds the writing or memorandum must be signed by the party to be charged or his agent.

_____ 8. The Parol Evidence Rule applies to all integrated written contracts and deals with what terms are part of the contract.

_____ 9. The Parol Evidence Rule is a rule of evidence that prohibits the parties from subsequently orally modifying their written contract.

_____ 10. Rules of contractual interpretation are incorporated within the Statute of Frauds.

Multiple Choice

_____ 1. The following promises or contracts are within the Statute of Frauds except

a. The promise of an executor or administrator that he personally will pay all of the decedent's creditors in full
b. A promise to marry made in consideration for some promise other than a reciprocal promise to marry
c. A promise made by a father to his son by which the father will pay the son's debt in the event of the son's default
d. A promise made by a father to his son's creditor to pay the son's debt in the event of his son's default

_____ 2. All of the following contracts are within the Statute of Frauds and therefore must meet its requirements in order to be enforceable except

a. a contract to sell one half acre lots of land in a 60 acre lot subdivision
b. a six month lease of an apartment
c. a deed granting an easement
d. a 30 year mortgage

_____ 3. A contract for the sale of securities (stocks and bonds) must be in writing to comply with the applicable Uniform Commercial Code Statute Frauds provision if the value of the securities involved exceeds

a. $50
b. $500
c. $5000
d. none of the above

_____ 4. All of the following are required of a writing to satisfy the requirements of the general contract Statute of Frauds except

a. It must be signed by the party to be charged or his agent
b. It must be signed by the party seeking to enforce the contract or his agent
c. It must specify the parties to the contract
d. It must specify with reasonable certainty the subject matter of the unperformed promises as well as their essential terms

_____ 5. Under the Statute of Frauds provision of the U.C.C. if a writing that is otherwise sufficient incorrectly states the quantity term agreed upon by the parties, the contract is

a. unenforceable
b. enforceable, but only to the extent of the quantity of goods stated in the writing
c. enforceable to the extent of the quantity term orally agreed upon by the parties
d. enforceable to the extent determined by the court to be fair and reasonable at the time of enforcement of the contract

_____ 6. An oral contract for the sale of land

a. is enforceable
b. is enforceable if the party seeking to enforce it has performed all of his promises under the oral contract
c. is enforceable if the party against whom enforcement is sought has performed all of his promises under the oral contract
d. is enforceable if all of the promises of the oral contract have been performed by all of the parties

_____ 7. If a contract is expressed in a writing that is intended by the parties to be the complete and final expression of their rights and and duties under the contract, the parol evidence rule precludes the admission into evidence of all of the following <u>except</u>

a. prior oral negotiations or agreements of the parties
b. prior written negotiations of the parties
c. a subsequent oral agreement between the parties to modify the terms of the contract
d. a contemporaneous oral agreement between the parties that varies or changes the written contract

_____ 8. The parol evidence will bar the introduction of

a. evidence that one of the parties to the contract was a minor
b. evidence of fraud in the formation of the contract
c. evidence of usage and custom that is not inconsistent with the terms of the written agreement
d. evidence of a letter written prior to the execution of the final contract stating that the price to be charged for the goods was \$2.00 each rather than \$2.10 as provided in the final contract

_____ 9. A party seeking to introduce evidence of a subsequent oral agreement modifying a written employment contract from 2 to 3 years would be

a. admissible under both the Statute of Frauds and the parol evidence rule
b. inadmissible because of the Statute of Frauds
c. inadmissible because of the parol evidence rule
d. inadmissible because of both the parol evidence rule and the Statute of Frauds

_____10. Which of the following is not a rule of interpretation?

a. Words and other conduct are interpreted in light of all the circumstances, and if the principal purpose is ascertainable it is given greater weight
b. Unless a different intention is manifested, technical terms and words of art are given their technical meaning
c. Express terms, usage of trade, course of dealing and course of performance are weighed in that order
d. Separately negotiated or added terms are given greater weight than standardized terms or other terms not separately negotiated

Short Essay

1. What is the difference between an original promise and a collateral promise?

2. Identify two instances in which a contract to transfer an interest in land need not be in writing and give an example of each?

3. Compare the requirements for a writing to comply with the general contract Statute of Frauds and the U.C.C. version. Which is easier to satisfy? Why? List four alternative methods of compliance with the U.C.C. version.

4. Identify six situations to which the Parol Evidence Rule does not apply.

12

RIGHTS OF THIRD PARTIES

Chapter Outline

I. Assignment of Rights and Delegation of Duties

  A. Assignment of Rights
    1. Requirements of an Assignment
      a. Definition
      b. Partial Assignments
    2. Rights that are Assignable
    3. Rights that are not Assignable
      a. Assignments that materially increase the risk or burden upon the obligor
      b. Assignments of personal rights
      c. Express prohibition against assignment
      d. Assignments prohibited by law
    4. Rights of the Assignee
      a. Implied warranties of assignor
      b. Notice
    5. Implied Warranties of Assignor
    6. Successive Assignments of the Same Right

  B. Delegation of Duties

II. Third Party Beneficiary Contracts

  A. Intended Beneficiary
    1. Gift Promise
    2. Creditor Beneficiary
    3. Rights of Intended Beneficiary

  B. Incidental Beneficiary

Definitions

1. Rights
2. Duties
3. Assignment of rights
4. Assignor
5. Assignee
6. Obligor
7. Delegation of duties
8. Delegator
9. Delegatee
10. Obligee
11. Partial assignment
12. Successive assignments
13. Third-party beneficiary contract
15. Intended beneficiary
16. Incidental beneficiary
17. Gift promise
18. Creditor beneficiary

True - False

_____ 1. An assignment of rights is a voluntary transfer to a third party of the rights arising from the contract.

_____ 2. After an effective assignment of rights, both the assignor and the assignee have a right to the obligor's performance.

_____ 3. After an effective delegation of duties, both the delegator and the delegatee are liable to the obligee for performance of the contractual duty.

_____ 4. Although no special words or particular form are necessary to create an assignment, an assignment must be supported by consideration to be effective.

_____ 5. For an assignment to be effective notice of the assignment must be given to the obligor.

_____ 6. A delegation of duties will not be permitted if the duties are of a personal nature.

_____ 7. Under the Restatement and the Code, unless the language or circumstances indicate otherwise, an assignment of "all my rights under the contract" is both an assignment of rights and a delegation of the assignor's duties under the contract.

_____ 8. A third party beneficiary contract usually is not enforceable by an incidental beneficiary.

_____ 9. A third party is an intended beneficiary if the promisee's purpose in bargaining for and obtaining the promisor's promise was to make a gift to the beneficiary.

_____10. The rights of an intended beneficiary vest at the time of the making of the contract or at the time he learns of its making, whichever is later.

_____11. In an action by the intended beneficiary of a third party beneficiary contract, the promisor may assert any defense that would have been available to him if the action had been brought by the promisee.

Multiple Choice

_____ 1. A gift assignment is

a. valid even though not supported by consideration
b. not revocable by the assignor
c. not terminated by the assignor's death
d. all of the above

_____ 2. A transfer of a portion of a person's rights under a contract to one or more assignees is called

a. a gift assignment
b. a revocable assignment
c. a partial assignment
d. none of the above

_____ 3. Which of the following assignments of contract rights are not valid

a. assignments that would materially increase the risk or burden on the obligor
b. assignments which would transfer a personal contract right
c. assignments which are prohibited by law
d. all of the above

_____ 4. An assignee of a contract

a. acquires all of the rights of the assignor
b. acquires new, additional rights by virtue of the assignment
c. takes the assigned rights free of all of the defenses to which the rights would be subject in an action by the assignor against the obligor
d. all of the above

_____ 5. For an assignment to be valid, notice of the assignment must be given to

a. the assignee
b. the assignor
c. the obligor
d. none of the above

_____ 6. In the absence of an expressed intention to the contrary, an assignor who receives value makes all of the following implied warranties to the assignee with respect to the assigned right except

a. that he will do nothing to defeat or impair the assignment
b. that the obligor will pay the assigned debt
c. that the assigned right actually exists
d. that he has no knowledge of any fact that would impair the value of the assignment

_____ 7. A delegation of contractual duties will not be permitted if

a. the duties are of a personal nature
b. the performance is expressly made non-delegable
c. the delegation is prohibited by statute or by public policy
d. all of the above

_____ 8. The delegator remains bound to perform his contractual duties even after a delegation unless the delegation is

a. a gratuitous delegation
b. a delegation for value
c. a novation
d. none of the above

_____ 9. A contract in which the promisor agrees to render a certain performance to a third person is called

a. a third party beneficiary contract
b. an assignment of rights
c. a delegation of duties
d. a novation

_____10. An intended creditor beneficiary of a third party beneficiary contract has rights against

a. the promisee/debtor only
b. the promisor only
c. both the promisee and the promisor
d. neither the promisee nor the promisor

Short Essay

1. Distinguish between an assignment of rights and a delegation of duties. How does an assignor's rights after an assignment differ from a delegator's duties after a delegation?

2. Although notice is not required for an assignment to be effective, why should notice of the assignment be given to the obligor?

3. What is the majority American rule regarding successive assignments of the same right? Identify the exceptions to that rule.

4. Distinguish between an intended creditor beneficiary and an intended gratuitous beneficiary. Against whom can each enforce his rights?

13

PERFORMANCE, BREACH AND DISCHARGE

<u>Chapter Outline</u>

A. Conditions

1. Express Conditions
2. Implied-in-Fact Conditions
3. Implied-in-Law Conditions
4. Concurrent Conditions
5. Conditions Precedent
6. Conditions Subsequent

B. Discharge By Performance

C. Discharge By Breach

1. Breach By One Party as a Discharge of the Other
   a. Material breach
   b. Substantial performance
2. Prevention of Performance
3. Anticipatory Repudiation
4. Material Alteration of Written Contract

D. Discharge by Agreement of the Parties

1. Mutual Rescission
2. Accord and Satisfaction
3. Novation

E. Discharge By Operation of Law

1. Subsequent Illegality
2. Impossibility
3. Bankruptcy
4. Statute of Limitations

Definitions

1. Discharge

2. Condition

3. Express condition

4. Implied-in-fact condition

5. Implied-in-law condition

6. Concurrent conditions

7. Condition precedent

8. Condition subsequent

9. Material breach

10. "Perfect Tender Rule"

11. Substantial performance

12. Anticipatory repudiation

13. Accord and satisfaction

14. Novation

True - False

_____ 1. A condition is any operative event the happening or non-happening of which affects one's duty of performance under a contract.

_____ 2. Even if a contract is expressly made subject to a subjective condition of satisfaction, courts generally will apply an objective, reasonable person standard to evaluate its performance.

_____ 3. In the absence of an agreement to the contrary, the law assumes that the respective performances under a contract are concurrent conditions.

_____ 4. A condition precedent is an operative event the happening of which terminates an existing duty of performance under a contract.

_____ 5. An uncured material breach by one party excuses the other's non-performance and discharges the aggrieved party from any further duty under the contract.

_____ 6. The Code has followed the common law doctrine of material breach in adopting the "Perfect Tender Rule".

_____ 7. A rescission must satsfy all of the essentials of an ordinary contract to be effective.

_____ 8. A promisor's good faith personal belief that she lacks the necessary capability or competence to perform her contractual duties will excuse her from liability for non-performance.

_____ 9. Under the Restatement and Code views of impossibility, commercial impracticability will excuse liability of non-performance.

_____10. In most States, the running of the period of the Statute of Limitations discharges the promisor's contractual liability.

Multiple Choice

_____ 1. A condition that is understood by the parties to be part of their agreement, but is not included in their express contract is called

a. an implied-in-law condition
b. an implied-in-fact condition
c. a concurrent condition
d. a condition precedent

_____ 2. An operative event that must take place before a duty of performance under the contract is created is called

a. an implied-in-law condition
b. a concurrent condition
c. a condition precedent
d. a condition subsequent

_____ 3. An uncured material breach of contract

a. gives rise to a cause of action for damages by the aggrieved party
b. operates as an excuse for non-performance by the aggrieved party
c. discharges the aggrieved party from any furhter duty under the contract
d. all of the above

_____ 4. The unjustified failure of one party to perform substantially the obligations of the contract constitutes

a. a perfect tender
b. a novation
c. a material breach
d. an accord

_____ 5. Which one of the following statements is not a correct principle to be applied in determining what constitutes a material breach

a. a failure to timely perform a promise is a material breach even if time is not of the essence
b. partial performance is a material breach if an essential part of the contract is not performed
c. if quantitatively significant, a breach will be considered material
d. an intentional breach of a contract is generally held to be material

_____ 6. If, prior to the date that performance is due, a party announces that he will not perform or commits an act that renders him unable to perform, he has committed

a. an anticipatory novation
b. an anticipatory repudiation
c. a prevention of performance
d. a material alteration of a written contract

_____ 7. An agreement between three parties to substitute a new promisee or promisor in place of an existing promisee or promisor is called

a. a condition subsequent
b. a mutual rescission
c. an accord and satisfaction
d. a novation

_____ 8. An agreement between the parties to a contract to terminate their respective duties under the contract is called

a. a novation
b. a mutual rescission
c. an accord and satisfaction
d. an anticipatory repudiation

_____ 9. A promisor will be excused from liability for failure to perform under a contract on grounds of impossibility when

a. she is financially unable to perform
b. she personally lacks the capability or competency to perform
c. no one, inculding the promisor, is able to perform
d. all of the above

_____10. The effect of a party's failure to bring an action before expiration of the period of the statute of limitations is

a. to discharge the promisor from liability
b. to act as a mutual rescission
d. to bar the remedy
d. to act as an accord and satisfaction

_____11. A contract in which the promisee agrees to accept and the promisor agrees to render a subsituted performance in satisfaction of an existing contractual duty is called

a. a material alteration of a written contract
b. an accord
c. a substantial performance
d. a novation

Short Essay

1. What is a condition? What is the difference between the breach of a promise and the failure of a condition?

2. At common law, when is a party excused from liability for non-performance of a contractual duty on grounds of impossibility? How have the Restatement and the Code altered this rule?

3. Explain the "perfect tender" rule and how it differs from the common law approach.

14

REMEDIES

Chapter Outline

A. Monetary Damages

1. Compensatory Damages
2. Reliance Damages
3. Foreseeability of Damages
4. Damages for Misrepresentation
   a. Fraud
   b. Non-fraudulent misrepresentation
5. Punitive Damages
6. Liquidated Damages
7. Mitigation of Damages

B. Remedies in Equity

1. Specific Performance
2. Injunctions

C. Restitution

1. Party Injured by Breach
2. Party in Default
3. Statute of Frauds
4. Voidable Contracts

D. Limitations on Remedies

1. Election of Remedies
2. Loss of Power of Avoidance
   a. Affirmance
   b. Delay
   c. Rights of third parties

Definitions

1. Compensatory damages

2. Reliance damages

3. Foreseeability of damages

4. "Out-of-pocket" damages

5. "Benefit-of-the-bargain" damages

6. Nominal damages

7. Punitive damages

8. Liquidated damages

9. Mitigation of damages

10. Specific performance

11. Injunction

12. Restitution

13. Incidental Damages

14. Consequential Damages

True - False

_____ 1. The primary objective of contract remedies is to compensate the injured party for the loss resulting from the contract breach by attempting to provide an equivalent of the promised performance.

_____ 2. An injured party may seek reliance damages as well as compensatory damages for a promisor's breach of contract.

_____ 3. Damages are recoverable for losses beyond those that the party in breach had reason to foresee as being a probable result of its breach when it entered into the contract.

_____ 4. The foreseeability of damages is a subjective test based on the breaching party's actual expectations.

_____ 5. Even if an unforeseeable, extraordinary loss results from a breach of contract, the injured party may still recover for any ordinary loss resulting from the breach.

_____ 6. Most States permit a party who has been induced to enter into a contract by fraud to recover only "out-of-pocket" damages.

_____ 7. Punitive damages are not recoverable for a breach of contract unless the breach also gives rise to a tort for which punitive damages are recoverable.

_____ 8. A contract provision by which the parties agree in advance to the damages to be paid in event of breach is enforceable even if it is not a reasonable forecast of the loss that would result from the breach.

_____ 9. When a breach of contract occurs, the injured party has a duty to take steps to minimize the damages that he may sustain.

_____ 10. Specific performance may be ordered even if monetary damages will provide an adequate remedy.

_____ 11. Restitution is the return to the injured party of the consideration that the injured party gave to the other party.

_____ 12. Under the doctrine of election of remedies, the injured party's choice of one available remedy will bar his choice of an additional, consistent remedy.

_____ 13. The power of avoidance may be lost if the party having the power does not rescind within a reasonable time.

Multiple Choice

_____ 1. The remedy which provides for damages to be awarded in an amount equal to the loss of value to the injured party caused by the other party's failure to perform or its deficient performance is called

a. compensatory damages
b. reliance damages
c. nominal damages
d. punitive damages

_____ 2. In computing reliance damages, which of the following expenses of the injured party are properly includible

a. expenses incurred in preparing to perform
b. expenses incurred in actually performing
c. the value of foregone opportunities to enter into another contract
d. all of the above

_____ 3. Money damages are only recoverable for losses that the party in breach had reason to foresee as a probable result of such breach at time that

a. the parties began negotiations
b. the parties entered into the contract
c. the breach occurred
d. none of the above

_____ 4. Acting in reliance on X's intentional misrepresentation as to a drill press's capabilities, Y purchased the press from X for $17,000. Although the value of the press if it had performed as promised would be $10,000, it's actual delivered value is $4,000. under the benefit-of-the-bargain rule, Y could recover

a. nothing
b. $3,000
c. $6,000
d. $7,000

_____ 5. Even if an injured party has not sustained or cannot prove an injury or loss resulting from a breach of contract, the injured party can still recover

a. compensatory damages
b. reliance damages
c. nominal damages
d. all of the above

_____ 6. A formal order issued by a court of equity commanding a party to render the performance promised under the contract is called

a. a decree of specific performance
b. an injunction
c. restitution
d. none of the above

_____ 7. In which of the following instances is restitution available as a remedy for breach of contract?

a. when one party totally fails to perform its obligations
b. when a party may not enforce the contract because of the Statute of Frauds
c. upon the avoidance of a voidable contract
d. all of the above

_____ 8. A party with a power of avoidance may lose that power if he

a. affirms the contract
b. delays unreasonably in exercising the power of disaffirmance
c. the rights of third parties intervene
d. all of the above

_____ 9. When a misrepresentation is innocent, the aggrieved party may recover damages under the

a. "out-of-pocket" damages rule
b. "benefit-of-the-bargain" damages rule
c. either (a) or (b)
d. neither (a) nor (b)

_____10. A liquidated damages provision will be enforced only if it is

a. a reasonable estimate of the loss that may result from the breach of contract
b. a reasonable estimate of the loss that actually results from the breach of contract
c. a substitute for a penalty
d. none of the above

Short Essay

1. Under what circumstances is a loss resulting from a breach of contract foreseeable and therefore recoverable by the injured party?

2. What is the doctrine of mitigation of damages? What will the effect be of the injured party's failure to take the appropriate steps?

3. What are the two major types of equitable remedies? Discuss each type, including an explanation of when each is available.

4. What is the remedy of restitution and when is it available?

15

INTRODUCTION TO SALES

Chapter Outline

I. Nature of Sales Contracts

A. Definition
B. Fundamental Principles of Article Two
1. Good Faith
2. Unconscionability
3. Expansion of Commerical Practices
4. Sales by and Between Merchants
5. Liberal Administration of Remedies
6. Freedom of Contract
7. Validation and Preservation of Sales Contracts

II. Formation of a Sales Contract

A. Manifestation of Mutual Assent
1. Definiteness of an Offer
a. Open price
b. Open delivery
c. Open quantity - output and requirements contracts
d. Other open terms
2. Firm Offers
3. Variant Acceptances
4. Auctions

B. Consideration
1. Contractual Modifications
2. Discharge of Claim After Breach
3. Firm Offers

C. Form of the Contract
   1. Statute of Frauds
      a. Modification of contracts within the Statute of Frauds
      b. Written compliance
      c. Alternative methods of compliance
   2. Parol Evidence
   3. Seal

Definitions

1. Sale

2. Goods

3. Bailment

4. Gift

5. Good faith

6. Unconscionability

7. Course of dealing

8. Usage of trade

9. Merchant

10. Firm offer

11. "Mirror image" rule

12. Auction without reserve

13. Parol evidence

True - False

_____ 1. A sale is defined as the transfer of title of goods from seller to buyer for a price.

_____ 2. Where general contract law has not been specifically modified by Article Two of the Code, principles of general contract law govern.

_____ 3. An employment contract is within the scope of Article Two.

_____ 4. The Code defines "unconscionability" as "fairness under the circumstances".

_____ 5. Most of the Code's provisions permit the parties to vary or displace them by agreement.

_____ 6. A merchant's firm offer is irrevocable for the stated period, not to exceed 3 months, even though no consideration is given to the merchant-offeror for that promise.

_____ 7. The Code has adopted the common law "mirror image" rule stating that an acceptance cannot deviate from the terms of the offer.

_____ 8. Under the Code, a unilateral offer must be accepted by a prompt shipment of the goods accompanied by notice to the buyer within a reasonable time.

_____ 9. Under the Code, a modification of an existing contract does not need to be supported by consideration to be binding.

_____10. A term specifying the quantity of goods sold is necessary for a writing to satisfy the Code's Statute of Fraud's compliance provision.

Multiple Choice

_____ 1. Which of the following transactions would be governed by Article Two of the Uniform Commercial Code?

a. the sale of a house
b. the sale of a typewriter
c. the lease of a typewriter
d. a contract of employment

_____ 2. A transfer of possession of goods without a transfer of title to them is called

a. a bailment
b. a sale
c. a gift
d. a lease

_____ 3. For a merchant, "good faith" requires

a. "honesty in fact in the conduct or transaction concerned"
b. "reasonable commercial standards of fair dealing in the trade"
c. neither (a) nor (b)
d. both (a) and (b)

_____ 4. A "merchant" is defined by the Code as a person

a. who is a dealer in the goods involved
b. who by his occupation holds himself out as having knowledge or skill peculiar to the goods or practices involved
c. who employs an agent or broker whom he holds out as having knowledge or skill peculiar to the goods or practices involved
d. all of the above

_____ 5. Most of the Code's provisions are not mandatory but instead permit the parties to vary or displace them, except

a. price
b. place of delivery
c. good faith
d. none of the above

_____ 6. Under the Code, if a merchant-seller's acceptance contains a term in addition to those contained in the non-merchant buyer's offer, the additional term is

a. ignored
b. construed as a proposal for an addition to the contract
c. construed as part of the contract even if it materially alters the agreement
d. construed as part of the contract unless the buyer expressly objects to its inclusion

_____ 7. Under the Code, which of the following requires consideration to be binding

a. a modification of an existing contract
b. a contract to sell goods
c. a written discharge of a claim after a breach of contract
d. a merchant's firm offer

_____ 8. In order to comply with the Code's version of the Statute of Frauds, the party seeking to enforce the contract must have a writing that is

a. notarized
b. signed by the party against whom enforcement is sought or by his authorized agent or broker
c. includes all material terms
d. all of the above

_____ 9. Under the Code, seals are effective with respect to

a. contracts for the sale of goods
b. offers to buy goods
c. offers to sell goods
d. none of the above

_____10. A practice or method of dealing regularly observed and followed in a place, vocation, or trade describes

a. a "usage of trade"
b. a "course of performance"
c. a "course of dealing"
d. an express term in a contract

Short Essay

1. When is Article Two of the Uniform Commercial Code applicaable? When is it inapplicable?

2. Compare the Code's position with that of the common law of contracts regarding the requisites of an effective acceptance of an offer.

3. Compare the obligation of "good faith" as imposed on merchants and non-merchants.

16

TRANSFER OF TITLE AND RISK OF LOSS

Chapter Outline

I. Transfer of Title and Other Property Rights

   A. Passage of Title
      1. Physical Movement of the Goods
         a. Shipment contract
         b. Destination contract
      2. No Movement of the Goods

   B. Other Property Rights
      1. Special Property
      2. Insurable Interest
      3. Security Interest

   C. Power to Transfer Title
      1. Void and Voidable Title to Goods
      2. Entrusting of Goods to a Merchant

II. Risk of Loss

   A. Risk of Loss in Absence of a Breach
      1. Agreement of the Parties
      2. Trial Sales
         a. Sale on approval
         b. Sale or return
         c. Consignment
      3. Contracts Involving Carriers
         a. Shipment contracts
         b. Destination contracts
      4. Goods in Possession of Bailee
      5. All Other Sales

B. Risk of Loss Where There is a Breach

1. Breach by the Seller
2. Breach by the Buyer

III. Sales of Goods in Bulk

A. Requirments of Article 6

B. Exempted Bulk Transfers

C. Effective Failure to Comply With Article 6

D. Application of the Proceeds

Definitions

1. Shipment contract

2. Destination contract

3. Special property

4. *Bona fide* purchaser

5. Entrustment

6. "Buyer in ordinary course of business"

7. Risk of loss

8. Sale on approval

9. Sale or return

10. Consignment

11. C.I.F.

12. C & F

13. C.O.D.

14. F.O.B.

15. Ex-ship

16. "No-arrival, no sale"

17. Bulk transfer

True - False

_____ 1. A transfer of title from seller to buyer is fundamental to the existence of a sale of goods.

_____ 2. Under a destination contract, title to the goods passes to the buyer at the time and place that the seller delivers the goods to the carrier.

_____ 3. Under the Code, only those persons with title to or a lien on goods have an insurable interest in those goods.

_____ 4. Any reservation by the seller of title to goods delivered to the buyer is the reservation of a security interest in those goods.

_____ 5. A seller may have the power but not the right to sell goods in his possession to certain buyers.

_____ 6. If a buyer with void title resells the goods to a *bona fide* purchaser for value and without notice of any flaw in his title, the *bona fide* purchaser acquires good title.

_____ 7. A "buyer in the ordinary course of business" is defined by the Code as one who acts honestly, gives value, and takes without notice or knowledge of any defect in the title of his transferor.

_____ 8. If risk of loss is placed on the seller, then he has no right to recover the purchase price for lost or damaged goods from the buyer.

_____ 9. Under both the common law and the Code, risk of loss is determined by ownership of the goods and whether title has been transferred.

_____ 10. Under the Code, risk of loss is allocated by the Code and an agreement by the parties to shift or divide the risk is not controlling.

_____ 11. In a sale on approval, risk of loss immediately passes to the buyer who retains title until he revests it in the seller by returning the goods.

_____ 12. Under the Code, a sale on consignment is regarded as a sale or return.

_____ 13. In a shipment contract, risk of loss passes to the buyer upon delivery of the goods to the carrier.

_____ 14. If a seller breaches a contract by shipping non-conforming goods to the buyer, risk of loss remains on the buyer until the buyer properly returns the goods to the seller.

_____15. A bulk transfer includes the sale of a merchant's inventory in the ordinary course of his business.

_____16. A transfer in bulk by way of security is exempt from the requirements of Article 6 of the Code.

Multiple Choice

_____ 1. A "destination contract" requires the seller to deliver the goods to a particular destination and title passes to the buyer

a. at the time and place that the seller delivers the goods to the carrier for shipment to the buyer's place of business
b. upon tender of the goods to the buyer at that destination
c. upon delivery of a document of title
d. at the time and place that the contract is entered into

_____ 2. A seller has an insurable interest in goods if

a. the goods have been identified as the goods to which the contract of sale refers
b. the seller has title to the goods
c. the seller has a security interest in the goods
d. all of the above

_____ 3. An interest in personal property or fixtures that secures payment or performance of an obligation is called

a. a security interest
b. a consignment
c. a bailment
d. title to the goods

_____ 4. In order to acquire good title to goods, a subsequent purchaser of goods from a transferee with voidable title must meet all of the following qualifications except
a. he must purchase the goods in good faith
b. he must purchase the goods after the original transferor rescinds the first transfer
c. he must purchase the goods for value
d. he must purchase the goods without notice of any infirmity of his title

_____ 5. Under the Code, a merchant entrusted with the possession of goods has the power to transfer good title to a buyer in the ordinary course of business if the entruster is

a. a thief
b. the owner of the goods
c. one who found the goods
d. all of the above

_____ 6. A transaction in which goods are sold and delivered to the buyer with an option to return them to the seller is called

a. a sale on approval
b. a sale or return
c. a bailment
d. a consignment

_____ 7. In a sale on approval, risk of loss passes to the buyer when

a. the contract is entered into by the parties
b. the goods are sent by the seller
c. the goods are received by the buyer
d. the goods are accepted by the buyer

_____ 8. In a shipment contract, risk of loss passes to the buyer when

a. the parties enter into the contract
b. the goods leave the seller's business
c. the goods are deliviered to a carrier
d. the goods are received by the buyer

_____ 9. Which, if any, of the following designations indicate that the contract is a shipment contract

a. F.O.B. place of shipment
b. F.A.S. port of shipment
c. C.I.F.
d. all of the above

_____10. In an ordinary contract in which the merchant-seller is required to tender or deliver the goods to a non-merchant buyer, risk of loss passes to the buyer

a. when the parties enter into the contract
b. upon the seller's tender of the goods to the buyer
c. when the buyer receives the goods
d. none of the above

_____11. If the seller ships non-conforming goods to the buyer, the risk of loss remains on the seller until

a. the buyer accepts the goods
b. the seller remedies the defect in the goods
c. either (a) or (b)
d. both (a) and (b)

_____12. A transfer in bulk is exempt from the requirements of Article 6 of the Code if

a. it is a transfer by way of security
b. it is a general assignment for the benefit of the creditors of the seller
c. it is a sale in the course of proceedings for the reorganization of a corporation in a court proceeding where notice is given to creditors
d. all of the above

Short Essay

1. Compare the significance of the concept of title under the common law with its role under the Code in allocating risk of loss.

2. What is the difference between a shipment and a destination contract? When does risk of loss pass to the buyer under each?

3. What is the differnece between void and voidable title? Of what significance is this difference in determining the rights of subsequent purchasers of the goods?

4. When does risk of loss pass to the buyer if the goods are held by a bailee and are to be delivered without being moved?

17

PERFORMANCE

Chapter Outline

I. Performance By the Seller

   A. Time and Manner of Deliverty
   B. Place of Tender
      1. Shipment contracts
      2. Destination contracts
      3. Goods held by bailee
   C. Quality of Tender
      1. Perfect tender rule
      2. Modifications of the perfect tender rule
         a. Agreement by the Parties
         b. Cure by the Seller
         c. Installment Contracts

II. Performance By The Buyer

   A. Inspection
   B. Rejection
   C. Acceptance
   D. Revocation of Acceptance
   E. Obligation of Payment

III. Execuses For Non-Performance

   A. Casualty to Identified Goods
   B. Non-Happening of Presupposed Conditions
   C. Substituted Performance

Definitions

1. Perfect tender rule

2. Cure

3. Inspection

4. Rejection

5. Acceptance

6. Revocation of acceptance

7. Substituted performance

True - False

_____ 1. In order for either party to a contract to maintain an action against the other party for non-performance of his contractual obligations, he must first put the other party into default.

_____ 2. Tender of delivery requires that the seller delivers the goods to the buyer's place of business.

_____ 3. Under the Code, the seller must tender all of the goods purchased under the contract in a single delivery and payment by the buyer is due on such tender, unless the parties specify otherwise in the contract.

_____ 4. If a contract does not identify the place for delivery of the goods, the place of delivery is the buyer's place of business; or if he has none, then the buyer's residence.

_____ 5. Under a shipment contract, the seller need only deliver the goods to a carrier and make a reasonable contract for their shipment.

_____ 6. Under the Code, the operation of the Perfect Tender Rule may not be limited by agreement of the parties to the contract.

_____ 7. If a buyer refuses a tender of non-conforming goods without informing the seller of the nature of the defect, he cannot then assert that defect as a breach of contract by the seller if the defect was curable.

_____ 8. If a non-conforming installment of goods substantially impairs the value of the whole contract, then the buyer can treat the breach of the installment as a breach of the whole contract.

_____ 9. Acceptance of any part of a commercial unit of goods operates as an acceptance of the entire unit.

_____10. If goods that were identified when the contract was made are totally or partially lost or damaged without fault of either party and before risk of loss passes to the buyer, the contract is avoided.

_____11. A party is not excused from his duty of performance under a contract upon the non-occurance of a presupposed condition unless that condition was a basic assumption underlying the contract.

Multiple Choice

_____ 1. A party may fulfill her contractual duty of performance and place the other party in default by all of the following except by

a. performing according to the contract
b. tendering her performance according to the contract
c. assuming that the other party will not perform according to the contract
d. being excused from tender of performance under the contract

_____ 2. Tender of conforming goods by the seller entitles him to

a. acceptance of the goods by the buyer
b. payment of the contract price by the buyer
c. both acceptance of the goods and payment of the contract price by the buyer
d. neither acceptance of the goods nor payment of the contract price by the buyer

_____ 3. Which of the following is not correct?

a. The seller has a duty to keep goods tendered for a period reasonably necessary for the buyer to take possession of them
b. Unless otherwise agreed, the buyer must furnish facilities reasonably suited to the receipt of the goods
c. Unless otherwise agreed, a contract is performable in installments
d. none of the above

_____ 4. If the contract does not specify the place for delivery of the goods, the place for deliverty is

a. the place of manufacture of the goods
b. the seller's place of business
c. the buyer's place of business
d. the carrier's place of business

_____ 5. Under a destination contract, the seller must do all of the following except

a. place the goods at the buyer's disposition at the specified destination
b. give the buyer reasonable notice to enable him to take delivery
c. tender the necessary documents of title if such documents are involved in the transaction
d. inspect the goods upon arrival at the specified destination to ensure that they are conforming

_____ 6. Under the Code, if the goods or the tender of deliverty fail to conform to the contract in any respect, the buyer may do any of the following except

a. reject the whole shipment
b. accept the whole shipment
c. accept as many commercial units as desired and reject the rest
d. none of the above

_____ 7. The buyer may reject non-conforming goods under the perfect tender rule except where

a. the parties agree to limit the buyer's right to reject non-conforming goods
b. the seller refuses to cure a non-conforming tender of delivery
c. the non-conformity of an installment does not substantilly impair the value of the whole contract
d. all of the above

_____ 8. Which of the following is an incorrect statement concerning a buyer's right to inspect goods upon delivery

a. Unless the parties agree otherwise, the buyer has the right to inspect the goods before payment or acceptance.
b. If the contract requires payment for the goods before acceptance, payment is required before inspection and operates as an acceptance of the goods.
c. The buyer may lose his right to reject or revoke acceptance of non-conforming goods if he fails to inspect them within a reasonable time.
d. The buyer must bear the expenses of inspection, but he may recover those costs from the seller if the goods prove to be non-conforming and are rejected.

_____ 9. After rejection of non-perishable goods, a merchant buyer that has received no instructions from the seller within a reasonable time after notice of rejection may

a. store the goods for the seller's account
b. reship the goods to the seller
c. resell the goods for the seller's account
d. all of the above

_____10. An effective acceptance occurs when the buyer

a. signifies to the seller that the goods conform to the contract
b. signifies to the seller that he will keep the goods
c. fails to make an effective rejection of the goods
d. all of the above

_____11. Acceptance of the goods precludes a buyer from

a. rejecting the goods
b. revoking his acceptance
c. suing the seller for breach for any non-conformity that could not be reasonably discovered by inspection
d. all of the above

_____12. If the goods contracted for are partially destroyed after risk of loss has passed to the buyer

a. the contract is avoided
b. the contract is voidable at the buyer's option
c. the contract is voidable at the seller's option
d. the contract is neither void nor voidable at either party's election

Short Essay

1. What are the basic performance obligations of the seller and buyer?

2. What must a seller do to discharge her obligation to tender delivery of the goods under a shipment contract?

3. What is meant by the doctrine of "cure"? When may a seller "cure" his defective tender or performance? Must the buyer accept the seller's cure?

4. What is the difference between a rejection and a revocation of acceptance? What are the buyer's rights under each?

5. Under what conditions can the parties to a contract be relieved of their obligations of full performance?

18

WARRANTIES AND PRODUCTS LIABILITY

Chapter Outline

I. Warranties

   A. Types of Warranties

      1. Express Warranties
      2. Warranty of Title
      3. Implied Warranties
         a. Merchantability
         b. Fitness for particular purpose

   B. Obstacles to Warranty Actions

      1. Disclaimer or Modification of Warranties
         a. Express exclusions
         b. Buyer's examination or refusal to examine
         c. Cumulation and conflict of warranties
         d. Federal legislation relating to warranties of consumer products
      2. Privity of Contract
         a. Horizontal privity
         b. Vertical privity
      3. Requirement of Notice of Breach
      4. Contributory Negligence
      5. Volunatry Assumption of the Risk

II. Strict Liability in Tort

A. Nature

1. Defective Condition
    a. Manufacturing defect
    b. Design defect
    c. Inadequate warning or instructions
2. Unreasonably Dangerous

B. Obstacles to Recovery
1. Disclaimers and Notice
2. Privity
    a. Horizontal privity
    b. Vertical privity
3. Plaintiff's Conduct
    a. Contributory negligence
    b. Comparative negligence
    c. Voluntary assumption of the risk
    d. Misuse or abuse of the product
4. Subsequent Alteration

Definitions

1. Warranty

2. Caveat emptor

3. Express warranty

4. Warranty of title

5. Implied warranties

6. Implied warranty of merchantability

7. Implied warranty of fitness for particular purpose

8. Disclaimer of warranties

9. Privity of contract

10. Strict liability in tort

True - False

_____ 1. A warranty may arise out of a seller's affirmation of fact, her promise, or from the circumstances under which the sale is made.

_____ 2. The Code requires that a seller's promise or affirmation of fact be relied upon by the buyer in order for it to constitute a warranty.

_____ 3. The Code's implied warranty of merchantability is applicable to all sales made by merchants

_____ 4. Application of the implied warranty of fitness for a particular purpose does not depend on whether the seller is a merchant.

_____ 5. The expression "as is" will only disclaim the implied warranty of merchantability if it is in writing and conspicuous.

_____ 6. Most states have eliminated the requirements of horizontal and vertical privity in warranty actions.

_____ 7. Strict liability in tort generally is not subject to disclaimer, exclusion, or modification by contractual agreement.

_____ 8. Strict liability in tort may arise from a manufacturing defect in the product but not from a mere defective design.

_____ 9. The strict liability in tort of manufacturers and other sellers extends only to buyers and their families.

_____10. The doctrine of strict liability in tort may be held to be applicable to merchant sellers of used goods.

_____11. Misuse or abuse of the product is an effective defense to a claim of strict liability in tort only if the misuse or abuse was not forseeable by the seller.

_____12. Under the Magnusor-Moss Act no seller providing a written warranty can effectively disclaim any implied warranty.

Multiple Choice

_____ 1. A promise made by the seller constitutes an express warranty provided

a. the buyer relied upon the promise
b. the promise constitutes a part of the basis of the bargain
c. either (a) or (b)
d. both (a) and (b)

_____ 2. An express warranty generally can arise from all of the following except

a. a model of the product shown to the buyer by the seller
b. a seller's promise as to the quality of the goods
c. an opinion as to the quality of the goods given by a non-expert seller
d. a seller's affirmation of fact as to specifications of the goods

_____ 3. In order for the implied warranty of fitness for a particular purpose to apply

a. the seller must, at the time of contracting, have reason to know of the particular purpose
b. the buyer must actually rely on the seller's skill and judgment to furnish suitable goods
c. either (a) or (b)
d. both (a) and (b)

_____ 4. Which of the following will not bar an injured buyer from recovering in an action against the seller for breach of warranty?

a. the buyer's failure to notify the seller of any breach of warranty within a reasonable time after he discovered it or should have discovered it
b. the buyer's contributory negligence
c. the buyer's voluntary assumption of the known risk
d. none of the above

_____ 5. The doctrine of strict liability in tort applies only if

a. the seller is engaged in the business of selling the product that caused the harm
b. the product as sold was in a defective condition unreasonably dangerous to the user or consumer
c. the product reaches the user or consumer without substantial change
d. all of the above

_____ 6. A party injured by a defective product can establish that it was defective by showing that the product had any of the following

a. a manufacturing defect
b. a design defect
c. inadequate instructions enclosed
d. all of the above

_____ 7. Strict liability in tort is applicable only if the product is

a. defective
b. somewhat dangerous to the user or consumer
c. either (a) or (b)
d. both (a) and (b)

_____ 8. An injured party's recovery under the doctrine of strict liability in tort will be barred by

a. a valid disclaimer of liability included in the contract of sale
b. the failure of the injured party to give notice to the seller within a reasonable time
c. subsequent alteration of the product
d. the lack of privity between the injured party and the seller

_____ 9. A party injured by a product that is defective because of a defective component can bring an action under the doctrine of strict liability in tort against all of the following <u>except</u>

a. the seller of the finished product
b. the assembler of the finished product
c. the manufacturer of a non-defective chassis to which the assembler attached the defective component
d. the manufacturer of the defective component used without essential change in the final product

_____ 10. Which of the following, even if properly shown is <u>not</u> a complete defense to a claim of strict liability in tort

a. comparative negligence
b. voluntary assumption of the risk
c. product misuse
d. all of the above

Short Essay

1. Under what circumstances does an opinion constitute an express warranty? Why?

2. Compare and contrast the implied warranties of merchantability and fitness for a particular purpose. Can either be disclaimed? How?

3. What must an injured party show to recover under a theory of strict liability in tort? What obstacles, if any, will bar his recovery and what traditional defenses will not?

19

REMEDIES

Chapter Outline

A. Remedies of the Seller

1. To Withhold Delivery of the Goods
2. To Stop Delivery of the Goods
3. To Identify Goods to the Contract
4. To Resell the Goods and Recover Damages
5. To Recover Damages for Non-acceptance or Repudiation
6. To Recover the Price
7. To Recover Incidental Damages
8. To Cancel the Contract
9. To Reclaim the Goods Upon Buyer's Insolvency

B. Remedies of the Buyer

1. To Cancel the Contract
2. To Recover Payments Made
3. To Cover
4. To Recover Damages for Non-delivery or Repudiation
5. To Recover Identified Goods Upon the Seller's Insolvency
6. To Sue for Replevin
7. To Sue for Specific Performance
8. To Obtain a Security Interest in the Goods
9. To Recover Damages for Breach in Regard to Accepted Goods
10. To Recover Incidental Damages
11. To Recover Consequential Damages

C. Contractual Provisions Affecting Remedies

1. Liquidation or Limitation of Damages
2. Modification or Limitation of Remedy

Definitions

1. Insolvency

2. Incidental damages

3. Cancellation

4. Cover

5. Consequential damages

6. Specific performance

7. Replevin

8. Liquidated damages

True - False

_____ 1. The purpose of the Code's remedial provisions is to place the aggrieved party in as good a position as if the other party had fully performed.

_____ 2. An "obligation oriented" remedy is one that provides the aggrieved party with the opportunity to recover monetary damages.

_____ 3. The Code has adopted the common law principle of election of remedies.

_____ 4. The aggrieved seller's right to stop delivery of goods by a carrier or other bailee upon learning of the buyer's insolvency ceases when a negotiable document of title covering the goods is negotiated to the buyer.

_____ 5. If a seller in good faith and in a commercially reasonable manner resells goods which were wrongfully rejected by the buyer, the seller may recover from the buyer the difference between the resale price and the contract price, plus any incidental damages incurred.

_____ 6. Goods resold by an aggrieved seller must be sold at a public sale.

_____ 7. The Code permits an aggrieved seller to bring an action to recover the price where the goods have been identified to the contract and there is no ready market available for their resale.

_____ 8. If a buyer breaches an installment contract in a manner that substantially impairs the whole contract, the seller may cancel the entire contract.

_____ 9. An aggrieved buyer may make a reasonable contract of cover and then seek to recover from the seller the difference between the cost of cover and the market price, plus any incidental and consequental damages.

_____ 10. In the event of a breach of warranty, the measure of damages is the difference, at the time and place of the acceptance of the non-conforming goods, between the value of the accepted goods and the value of the goods as warranted.

_____ 11. A contract provision limiting consequential damages for commercial losses resulting from a breach of warranty in the sale of goods is on its face unconscionable.

Multiple Choice

_____ 1. Which of the following is not a money-oriented remedy?

a. cover or resale and recover damages
b. an action to recover market price damages
c. cancellation
d. an action to recover damages for non-conformity

_____ 2. Under the Code, the equity meaning of insolvency is

a. that a person has no assets
b. that a person is unable to pay her debts as they become due
c. that a person's total liabilities exceed the value of all her assets
d. none of the above

_____ 3. A seller may withhold delivery of goods to a buyer who has breached their contract by

a. wrongfully rejecting the goods
b. failing to make a payment due on or before delivery
c. repudiating the contract
d. all of the aove

_____ 4. A seller may not recover market price damages if the buyer

a. wrongfully rejects the goods
b. wrongfully revokes his acceptance of the goods
c. fails to make a payment when due
d. none of the above

_____ 5. In the event of the buyer's wrongful repudiation of the contract, the seller may recover damages measured by the difference between the unpaid contract price and the market price at the time and place

a. that the goods were tendered by the seller
b. that the buyer repudiated the contract
c. that the contract was entered into
d. none of the above

_____ 6. The Code permits the seller to bring an action to recover the price in all of the following cases except

a. where the buyer has accepted the goods but has failed to make a payment
b. where the goods have been identified to the contract and a ready market is available for their resale at a reasonable price
c. Where conforming goods have been lost or damaged after risk of loss has passed to the buyer
d. all of the above

_____ 7. If an aggrieved pary rightfully cancels a contract

a. he discharges any obligation of future performance that he might have under the contract
b. he retains any remedy for breach of the whole contract or of any unperformed balance
c. neither (a) or (b)
d. both (a) and (b)

_____ 8. Which of the following is <u>not</u> a correct statement concerning an unpaid seller's attempt to recalim goods from an insolvent buyer

a. The seller must demand that the goods be returned within twenty days after the buyer has received them unless the buyer has fraudulently misrepresented his solvency to the seller.
b. The seller, if successful in reclaiming the goods from an insolvent buyer, may not seek other remedies with respect to the goods
c. The seller's right to reclaim the goods is subject to the rights of a buyer in the ordinary course of business or other good faith purchase
d. all of the above

_____ 9. If a seller tenders non-conforming goods and the buyer accepts them and then can not justifiably revoke his acceptance, the buyer can still

a. recover damages for non-conformity
b. recover market price for damages
c. neither (a) nor (b)
d. both (a) and (b)

_____10. If the buyer rightfully rejects the seller's tender of non-coforming goods, he may

a. cover and recover damages
b. recover payments made
c. recover market price damages
d. all of the above

_____11. If the seller repudiates the contract, the buyer is entitled to recover damages from the seller in an amount equal to the difference between the contract price and the market price of goods when

a. the parties entered into the contract
b. the breach occurred
c. the buyer learned of the breach
d. none of the above

_____12. X contracted to buy 1000 widgets from Y for $5,000. Y shipped defective widgets, but X accepted them and properly notified Y of the breach. As warranted, the widgets were valued at $7,000, but as received they were worth $4,000. If X is successful in his suit for breach of warranty against Y, he will be allowed to recover

a. $1,000
b. $2,000
c. $3,000
d. $7,000

Short Essay

1. What remedies are available to a buyer who rightfully rejects a seller's tender of non-conforming goods?

2. What remedies are available to a buyer after the seller repudiates their contract?

3. What remedies are available to the seller after the buyer has wrongfully rejected a conforming tender of goods?

4. Under what conditions may the parties to a contract limit or modify the remedies available for its breach?

20

FORM AND CONTENT

Chapter Outline

A. Negotiability

B. Types of Commercial Paper

1. Order to Pay
    a. Drafts
    b. Checks
2. Promises to Pay
    a. Notes
    b. Certificates of Deposit

C. Form of Commercial Paper

1. Writing
2. Signed
3. Promise or Order to Pay Money
4. Unconditional
    a. Reference to other agreements
    b. The particular fund doctrine
5. Sum Certain in Money
    a. Money
    b. Sum certain
6. No Other Promise or Order
7. Payable on Demand or at a Definite Time
    a. "On or before" clauses
    b. At a fixed period after a stated date
    c. At a fixed period after sight
    d. At a definite time subject to acceleration
    e. At a definite time subject to extension

8. Payable to Order or to Bearer
    a. Payable to order
    b. Payable to bearer
9. Terms and Ommissions and Their Effect on Negotiability
    a. Absence of statement of consideration
    b. Absence of statement of where the instrument is drawn or payable
    c. Sealed instruments
    d. Dating of the instrument
    e. Incomplete instruments
    f. Ambiguous instruments

Definitions

1. Commercial paper

2. Check

3. Draft

4. Promissory note

5. Certificate of deposit

6. Negotiability

7. Drawer

8. Drawee

9. Payee

10. Maker

11. Order paper

12. Bearer paper

True - False

_____ 1. A draft may be handwritten on a napkin.

_____ 2. An instrument is non-nogotiable if it is payable in a foreign currency.

_____ 3. An instrument in which no time for payment is stated is payable on demand.

_____ 4. An instrument is non-negotiable if the obligor may extend the maturity of the instrument for a definite period of time.

_____ 5. An instrument is non-negotiable if the holder may extend the maturity of the instrument for an indefinite period of time.

_____ 6. An instrument may be payable to two or more payees.

_____ 7. An instrument, otherwise negotiable, is negotiable bearer paper if by its terms it is payable to "cash".

_____ 8. An instrument is non-negotiable if it is incomplete

_____ 9. An instrument may be payable to the maker or drawer.

_____10. In resolving ambiguities, printed words control typewritten and handwritten words, and typewritten words control handwritten words.

Multiple Choice

_____ 1. If a negotiable instrument is not payable on demand, it can not be

a. a draft
b. a check
c. a promissory note
d. a certificate of deposit

_____ 2. A check must be signed by

a. the drawer
b. the drawee
c. the payee
d. the maker

_____ 3. A promissory note must be signed by

a. the drawer
b. the drawee
c. the payee
d. the maker

_____ 4. A signature on an instrument may

a. appear in the upper right hand corner
b. be a thumbprint
c. be an assumed name
d. all of the above

_____ 5. An instrument is non-negotiable if it

a. refers to the existence of a separate agreement
b. states that it is subject to the terms of a separate agreement
c. is attached to a separate agreement
d. is made payable the "assigns of Richard Roe"

_____ 6. An instrument is non-negotiable if it

a. relies upon the general credit of the drawer or maker
b. directs that a particular account be debited after payment
c. directs that payment be made out of a particular fund
d. states that it is given in consideration for the purchase of a blue suit

_____ 7. An instrument is non-negotiable if it

a. is payable with interest "at current rate"
b. provides for the recovery of costs and attorney's fees upon default
c. is payable with a fixed addition if paid after maturity
d. is payable at a stated rate of interest which will increase by 2% upon default

_____ 8. An instrument is non-negotiable if it

a. contains a promise or order to pay 800 French francs
b. provides that the payee, by cashing it, acknowledges full satisfaction of an obligation of the drawer
c. contains a promise to deliver goods
d. contains a promise to maintain collateral in case of a default in payment

_____ 9. An instrument is non-negotiable if

a. it is payable upon an event uncertain as to time of occurence
b. it is undated and payable 90 days after date
c. the obligor may extend the maturity of the instrument for an indefinite period of time
d. all of the above

_____10. An instrument is non-negotiable if it is payable

a. to bearer
b. to Richard Roberts
c. to the order of Richard Roberts
c. to the order of Richard Roberts or bearer

Short Essay

1. Can a check be converted to a time instrument? Explain.

2. Is the following instrument "I.O.U., Adam Brown $100, /s/ Joe Green" negotiable? Explain.

3. List the 8 requisites for an instrument to be negotiable.

21

TRANSFER

<u>Chapter Outline</u>

A. Transfer and Negotiation

B. Indorsements

1. Blank Indorsements
2. Special Indorsements
3. Restrictive Indorsements
   a. Conditional indorsements
   b. Indorsements prohibiting further transfer
   c. Indorsements for deposit or collection
   d. Indorsements in trust
4. Qualified Indorsements

Definitions

1. Holder

2. Negotiation

3. Assignment

4. Indorsement

5. Qualified indorsement

6. Blank indorsement

7. Special indorsement

8. Restrictive indorsement

True - False

_____ 1. A non-negotiable instrument is not transferable.

_____ 2. An indorsement written on a piece of paper clipped to the instrument is not negotiable.

_____ 3. An instrument may have no "holder".

_____ 4. A negotiable instrument may only be transferred by negotiation.

_____ 5. A negotiable instrument may only be negotiated by a holder.

_____ 6. Forging the signature of an accommodation indorser breaks the chain of title to the instrument.

_____ 7. Forging the signature of an indorsee breaks the chain of title to the instrument.

_____ 8. A qualified indorsement destroys the instrument's negotiability.

_____ 9. An instrument may have more than one holder at a time.

_____ 10. A restrictive indorsement prevents further negotiation of the instrument.

Multiple Choice

_____ 1. Indorsement by the appropriate parties is necessary to

a. transfer an instrument by assignment
b. negotiate a bearer instrument
c. negotiate an order instrument
d. (a) and (c) but not (b)

_____ 2. To be a holder of a bearer instrument requires

a. a transfer for value
b. possession of the instrument
c. the indorsement of the transferor
d. all of the above

_____ 3. Order paper may be converted into bearer paper by

a. a blank indorsement
b. a special indorsement
c. a restrictive indorsement
d. a qualified indorsement

_____ 4. Negotiability is destroyed if an instrument is indorsed with the words

a. "pay to A only"
b. "pay to the order of A"
c. "pay to A or his order"
d. none of the above

_____ 5. An indorsement is ineffective as a negotiation if it

a. is not dated
b. conveys only the unpaid balance on the instrument
c. is forged
d. (b) and (c) but not (a)

_____ 6. Bearer paper may be converted into order paper by

a. a blank indorsement
b. a special indorsement
c. a restrictive indorsement
d. a qualified indorsement

_____ 7. If H, the holder of a note, indorses it, "Pay A, but only if P is elected President in November," the indorsement is

a. blank - restrictive - qualified
b. special - non-restrictive - qualified
c. blank - non-restrictive - unqualified
d. special - restrictive - unqualified

_____ 8. An indorsement which reads "Pay only if the goods are delivered by December 1, without recourse, Jane Jones" is

a. blank - non-restrictive - qualified
b. blank - restrictive - unqualified
c. blank - restrictive - qualified
d. special - restrictive - unqualified

_____ 9. Which of the following is an example of an effective restrictive indorsement?

a. "pay A only"
b. "pay any bank"
c. "pay XYZ bank"
d. "pay A, without recourse"

_____10. If a note is conditionally indorsed, then the indorsee

a. is entitled to payment unless the condition fails
b. has no rights in the instrument regardless of the outcome, because a promise to pay must be unconditional
c. is entitled to payment, regardless of the outcome, because a promise to pay must be unconditional
d. none of the above

Short Essay

1. Is it a good idea to send bearer paper by mail? Explain.

2. List and describe the various types of indorsements.

22

HOLDER IN DUE COURSE

Chaper Outline

A. Requirements of a Holder in Due Course

    1. Holder
    2. Value
    3. Good Faith
    4. Lack of Notice
        a. Notice of a claim or defense
        b. Notice an instrument is overdue
        c. Notice an instrument has been dishonored

B. Holder in Due Course Status

    1. A Payee May be a Holder in Due Course
    2. The Shelter Rule

C. The Preferred Position of a Holder in Due Course

    1. Real Defenses
        a. Minority
        b. Void obligations
        c. Fraud in the execution
        d. Discharge in insolvency proceedings
        e. Discharge of which the holder has notice
        f. Forgery and unauthorized signature
        g. Material alteration
    2. Personal Defenses

D. Limitations Upon Holder in Due Course Rights

Definitions

1. Holder in due course

2. Value

3. Material alteration

4. Notice

5. Shelter rule

6. Real defense

7. Personal defense

True - False

_____ 1. A transferee of a negotiable instrument may acquire greater rights than his transferor had.

_____ 2. A person may acquire the rights of a holder in due course even though he does not take the instrument for value.

_____ 3. A holder takes an instrument for value only when he pays the face amount of the instrument.

_____ 4. A check is presumed overdue if it has been outstanding more than 30 days.

_____ 5. A payee may be a holder in due course.

_____ 6. Real defenses may not be asserted against a holder in due course.

_____ 7. A person may be a holder in due course even if he takes the instrument after all of the parties to the instrument have been discharged regardless of whether or not he has notice of the discharge.

_____ 8. When an incomplete instrument has been completed in an unauthorized manner, a subsequent holder may enforce the instrument according to the authority actually given, even though the completion has the effect of changing the contract of the previous signers.

_____ 9. When an incomplete instrument has been completed in an unauthorized manner, a subsequent holder in due course may enforce the instrument as completed.

_____10. Under the FTC's holder in due course rule, the buyer may have a defense against the holder even though the buyer has no defense against the seller.

Multiple Choice

_____ 1. A person may be a holder in due course if he takes the instrument

a. for value
b. in bad faith
c. with notice that it has been dishonored
d. all of the above

_____ 2. A person may acquire the rights of a holder in due course if he takes the instrument

a. for value
b. in bad faith
c. with notice that it has been dishonored
d. all of the above

_____ 3. A holder takes an instrument for value when he

a. makes an irrevocable commitment to his transferor
b. promises to pay the agreed consideration
c. takes the instrument as security for an antecedent debt
d. (a) and (c) but not (b)

_____ 4. A purchaser takes an instrument in good faith if

a. he believes there is nothing wrong with it
b. he knows there is something wrong with it
c. a prudent man under the circumstance would not have known that something was wrong with it, but the purchaser in fact knows something is wrong with it
d. (a) and (c) but not (b)

_____ 5. A holder has knowledge of a claim or defense if

a. the instrument has been undetectably altered
b. he knows that one or more of the parties to the instrument have been discharged
c. he knows that all the parties to the instrument have been discharged
d. all of the above

_____ 6. Assume M issues a note to P which is successively negotiated to A, B, C, and H. If H is a holder in due course with respect to all the parties to the instrument, then H is subject to the personal defenses of

a. A only
b. B only
c. C only
d. none of the above

_____ 7. Assume M issues a note to P which is successively negotiated to A, B, C, and H. If H is a holder in due course with respect to all the parties to the instrument, then H is subject to the real defenses of

a. A only
b. B only
c. C only
d. all of the above

_____ 8. A party to an instrument has a real defense if his obligation on the instrument

a. is void
b. is voidable
c. has been discharged
d. is the result of fraud in the inducement

_____ 9. A forged signature operates as the signature of

a. the person whose name is forged
b. the forger
c. any person who takes the instrument with notice that the signature has been forged
d. none of the above

_____10. Under the FTC's holder in due course rule, the consumer buyer may successfully assert

a. real defenses
b. personal defenses
c. real and personal defenses
d. none of the above

Short Essay

1. Who may be a holder in due course?

2. Why is it so important to be considered a holder in due course?

3. Most payees do not enjoy the rights of a holder in due course. Why?

4. Suppose you are on your way out to do some shopping when your roommate hands you a list of a few things she would like you to pick up. She gives you a blank check to pay for them. Can you legally spend that check?

23

LIABILITY OF PARTIES

Chapter Outline

I. Contractual Liability

A. Signature

1. Authorized Signatures
2. Unauthorized Signatures

B. Liability of Primary Parties

1. Makers
2. Acceptors

C. Liability of Secondary Parties

1. Indorsers and Drawers
2. Conditions Precedent to Liability
   a. Presentment
   b. Notice of dishonor
   c. Protest
   d. Delay in presentment, notice, or protest excused
   e. Presentment, notice, or protest excused
   f. Presentment excused
   g. Waiver of presentment, notice, or protest
3. Disclaimer of Liability by Secondary Parties

D. Liability of Accommodation Parties

E. Liability of Parties for Conversion

F. Special Situations Affecting Liability

1. The Importer Rule
2. The Fictitious Payee Rule

II. Liability Based on Warranty

A. Warranties or Transfer

1. Good Title
2. Signatures Genuine
3. No Material Alteration
4. No Defenses
5. No Knowledge of Insolvency

B. Warranties on Presentment

1. Good Title
2. Genuineness of Signature of Maker and Drawer
3. Material Alteration

III. Termination of Liability

A. Payment or Satisfaction

B. Tender of Payment

C. Cancellation and Renunciation

D. Impairment of Recourse or Collateral

E. Other Methods of Discharge

Definitions

1. Acceptance
2. Certification
3. Presentment
4. Dishonor
5. Protest
6. Secondary liability
7. Discharge
8. Accommodation party
9. Conversion
10. Transferor's warranty
11. Presenter's warranty
12. Primary liability

True - False

_____ 1. A person may be liable on a negotiable instrument even if he doesn't sign it.

_____ 2. A forger will be liable on an instrument even though he signs someone else's name and not his own.

_____ 3. A bank must honor a check drawn upon it.

_____ 4. A delay in presentment of a check discharges the drawer, irrespective of any showing of loss

_____ 5. The holder of a dishonored check may not sue the drawer if it involves skipping intermediate indorsers.

_____ 6. A bank that pays an instrument on a forged indorsement will not be liable for conversion if it acted in good faith.

_____ 7. Under the imposter rule, the indorsement of any person in the name of the named payee is effective as the indorsement of the named payee.

_____ 8. An indorser may disclaim warranty liability

_____ 9. If an instrument is transferred by delivery alone (without indorsement) warranties in transfer run to the immediate transferee only.

_____10. An unreasonable delay in presentment of a check discharges an indorser, irrespective of any showing of loss.

_____11. A maker may be liable on a note even though he has already paid the holder.

Multiple Choice

_____ 1. A signature may be

a. printed
b. made by an authorized agent
c. typed
d. all of the above

_____ 2. A drawee bank becomes liable on a check when

a. the check is written
b. the drawer issues the check
c. the payee indorses the check
d. the bank accepts the check

_____ 3. An indorser may disclaim contractual liability on an instrument if his indorsement contains the words

a. "time is of the essence"
b. "Caveat Emptor"
c. "without recourse"
d. "notice of dishonor"

_____ 4. The holder of an instrument has an immediate right of recourse against drawers and indorsers upon

a. proper presentment
b. dishonor
c. proper presentment and dishonor
d. proper presentment, dishonor, and notice of dishonor

_____ 5. Presentment and notice may be excused where the party to be charged

a. has himself dishonored the instrument
b. has himself counteracted payment
c. has no reason to expect the instrument to be accepted or paid
d. all of the above

_____ 6. If A, B, and C indorse a note, in that order, as accommodation parties for the same individual, who will ultimately bear the loss upon the maker's default?

a. A only
b. B only
c. C only
d. A, B, and C will share the loss equally

_____ 7. Which of the following is <u>not</u> a warranty of transfer

a. no material alteration
b. maker is solvent
c. good title
d. signatures genuine

_____ 8. A drawee bank can recover from the person who obtains payment of a check if

a. the drawer's signature is forged
b. the payee's signature is forged
c. the amount is raised after the check has been certified
d. none of the above

_____ 9. Which of the following is <u>not</u> an example of conversion?

a. a drawee to whom a draft is delivered for acceptance refuses to return it on demand
b. an instrument is paid on a forged indorsement
c. a holder unjustifiably impairs any collateral given on an instrument by a party to that instrument
d. a drawee to whom an instrument is delivered for payment refuses on demand either to pay or to return it

_____10. A holder who strikes out an indorser's signature

a. has discharged that indorser
b. is liable for conversion
c. has broken the chain of title
d. is not entitled to payment

_____11. An indorser who is required to pay an instrument has <u>no</u> right of recourse against

a, subsequent indorsers
b. prior indorsers
c. makers and acceptors
d. any party

Short Essay

1. Can a drawee bank recover payments made on some forged or altered instruments? Explain.

2. If your roommate writes you a check for his or her share of the monthly telephone bill, and it is dishonored by the bank, how concerned should you be about giving the required notice of dishonor? Is your roommate discharged if you unreasonably delay in giving the notice?

3. What are the differences between primary and secondary liability?

4. When is a drawee liable?

24

BANK DEPOSITS AND COLLECTIONS

Chapter Outline

A. Collection of Items

1. Collecting Banks
    a. Duty of care
    b. Duty to act seasonably
    c. Indorsements
    d. Warranties
    e. Final payment

x 2. Payor Banks

B. Relationship Between Payor Bank and Its Customer

1. Payment of an Item
2. Stop Payment Orders
3. Effect of Customer's Death or Incompetence
4. Customer's Duties

C. Electronic Fund Transfer

1. Types of Electronic Fund Transfer
    a. Automated teller machines
    b. Point-of-sale systems
    c. Direct deposits and withdrawals
    d. Pay-by-phone systems
2. Electronic Fund Transfer Act
    a. Disclosure
    b. Documentation and periodic statements
    c. Error resolution
    d. Consumer Liability
    e. Liability of financial institution

Definitions

1. Depositary bank

2. Payor bank

3. Intermediary banks

4. Collecting bank

5. Provisional credit

6. Final payment

7. Midnight deadline

8. Stop payment order

9. Automated teller machines

10. Point-of-sale systems

11. Preauthorized transfer

True - False

_____1. A provisional credit becomes final when the amount of the check has been paid by the drawee

_____2. A collecting bank is strictly liable for mishandling an item transferred to it for collection.

_____3. Once a check is restrictively indorsed, only a bank may acquire the rights of a holder.

_____4. A payor bank which dishonors an item must either return the item or send written notice of dishonor before midnight of the banking day on which the item is received.

_____5. A bank may pay its customer's check and charge her account for the full amount even though there are insufficient funds in her account to cover the check.

_____6. A bank may refuse to pay its customer's check even though there are sufficient funds in his account to cover the check.

_____7. A bank is required to dishonor its customer's check if the check is over six months old.

_____8. A bank may pay a check drawn by its customer even though the bank knows of the death of the customer.

_____9. A consumer's liabilty for unauthorized electronic fund transfer is limited to $100 if the consumer notifies the financial institution within two days after she learns of the loss.

_____10. Point-of-sale systems enable a consumer automatically to transfer funds from his bank to a merchant seller.

Multiple Choice

_____1. If a check is not paid for any reason, the payor bank should

a. return it to the drawer
b. return it to the drawee
c. return it to its transferor
d. throw it away

_____2. A depositary bank may treat a check as having been received on Monday if the check was actually received late in the afternoon on

a. Tuesday
b. Wednesday
c. Thursday
d. Friday

_____3. In presenting an item for payment, a collecting bank may delay presentment for up to

a. one calendar day
b. one banking day
c. three banking days
d. one week

_____4. Which of the following is responsible for examining a check for prior restrictive indorsements?

a. the depositary bank
b. the intermediary banks
c. the payor bank
d. all of the above

_____5. Final payment of an item occurs during the processing of the item by

a. the depositary bank
b. the intermediary banks
c. the payor bank
d. none of the above

_____6. Assume D issues several checks which are received by the payor bank on the same day. If there are insufficient funds in D's account to cover all the checks, the bank must pay the checks

a. in any order it deems convenient
b. in the order they were issued
c. in the order they were received
d. in the order specified by the drawer

_____7. A bank may dishonor a check without incurring a liability to its customer from whose account the item should have been paid if

a. payment of the check has been stopped by the drawer
b. the check is over six months old
c. the signature on the check is forged
d. all of the above

_____8. An oral stop payment order

a. is not valid
b. is valid for 7 days
c. is valid for 14 days
d. is valid for 6 months

_____9. A written stop payment order

a. is valid for 60 days
b. is valid for 90 days
c. may be renewed in writing
d. (a) and (c) but not (b)

_____10. If a consumer does not report the loss or theft of his electronic fund transfer card within two days he is liable for losses up to

a. $500
b. $250
c. $50
d. any unauthorized use

Short Essay

1. Suppose your roommate writes you a check for his or her share of the monthly phone bill. Do you have to indorse the check when you deposit it? Explain.

2. If a bank honors its customer's stop payment order, is he automatically relieved of liability on the check? Explain.

25

Agency and Employment Relationship

Chapter Outline

I. Agency Relationship

A. Nature of Agency

1. Definition
2. Scope of Agency Purposes
3. Other Legal Relations

B. Creation of Agency

1. Formalities
2. Capacity
   a. Capacity to be a principal
   b. Capacity to be an agent

C. Duties of Agent to Principal

1. Duty of Obedience
2. Duty of Diligence
3. Duty to Inform
4. Duty to Account
5. Fiduciary Duty

D. Duties of Principal to Agent

1. Contractual Duties
   a. Compensation
   b. Reimbursement
   c. Indemnification
2. Tort Duties

E. Termination of Agency

1. Acts of the Parties
    a. Mutual agreement of the parties
    b. Fulfillment of purpose
    c. Revocation of authority
    d. Renunciation by the agent
2. Operation of Law
    a. Bankruptcy
    b. Death
    c. Incapacity
    d. Change in business conditions
    e. Loss or destruction of the subject matter
    f. Loss of qualification of principal or agent
    g. Disloyalty of agent
    h. Change of law
    i. Outbreak of war
3. Irrevocable Agencies

II. Employment Relationship

A. Labor Law

1. Norris - La Guardia Act
2. National Labor Relations Act
3. Labor - Management Relations Act
4. Labor - Management Reporting and Disclosure Act

B. Employment Discrimination Law

1. Equal Pay Act
2. Civil Rights Act of 1964
3. Age Discrimination in Employment Act of 1967
4. Rehabilitation Act of 1973
5. Executive Order

C. Employee Safety

1. Occupational Safety and Health Act
2. Worker's Compensation

Definitions

1. Agent

2. Principal

3. Employee

4. Independent contractor

5. Diligence

6. Fiduciary duty

7. Reimbursement

8. Indemnification

9. Irrevocable agency

10. Labor dispute

11. Collective bargaining

12. Unfair labor practices

13. Union unfair practices

14. Affirmative action

15. Fellow servant rule

True - False

_____ 1. An agency relationship may only be created by contract.

_____ 2. An agent who is incompetent to bind himself by contract may not make a contract which is binding on his principal.

_____ 3. An agent is under a duty to keep her principal's property separate from her own.

_____ 4. A principal is under no duty to reimburse his agent for unauthorized expenses incurred by the agent.

_____ 5. An agent may make a contract which is binding on his principal even though the principal has terminated the agent's authority.

_____ 6. A Federal court may issue a civil injunction in a nonviolent labor dispute where there is an unfair labor practice.

_____ 7. A union may not take disciplinary action against a union member.

_____ 8. The Equal Pay Act prohibits an employer from discriminating between employees on the basis of race, color, sex, religion or national origin by paying unequal wages for equal work.

_____ 9. In a worker's compensation proceeding, the amounts recoverable for each type of injury are fixed by statute.

_____ 10. An injured employee may demand a jury trial even though he qualifies for worker's compensation.

Multiple Choice

_____ 1. A person may ordinarily appoint an agent to

a. perform a contract for personal services
b. commit an illegal act
c. negotiate the terms of a contract for personal services
d. (a) and (c) but not (b)

_____ 2. Any contracts resulting from the appointment of an agent by a minor are

a. void
b. voidable
c. unenforceable
d. none of the above

_____ 3. An agent may not ordinarily represent her principal in an transaction in which

a. she has a personal interest
b. she is acting on behalf of a competitor of her principal
c. she is acting on behalf of anyone whose interests conflict with those of her principal
d. all of the above

_____ 4. Assume that S wants to sell his house and B is interested in buying it. If A is an agent who normally handles such transactions, A may represent

a. S or B, but not both
b. S and B, but only with the informed consent of S
c. S and B, but only with the informed consent of B
d. S and B, but only with the informed consent of S and B

_____ 5. Where the agent has an interest in the subject matter of the agency, the agent's authority is terminated by

a. the death of the principal
b. the bankruptcy of the principal
c. a revocation of authority
d. the mutual agreement of the parties

_____ 6. An employer who refuses to bargain in good faith with the duly established representatives of his employees has violated

a. the Norris La Guardia Act
b. the National Labor Relations Act
c. the Labor Management Relations Act
d. the Labor Management Reporting and Disclosure Act

_____ 7. A union which goes on strike to force an employer to fire a non-union employee has violated

a. the Norris - La Guardia Act
b. the National Labor Relations Act
c. the Labor Management Relations Act
d. the Labor Management Reporting and Disclosure Act

_____ 8. The Act which prohibits discrimination on the basis of handicap in programs receiving Federal financial assistance is

a. the Rehabilitation Act of 1973
b. the Civil Rights Act of 1964
c. the Age Discrimination in Employment Act of 1976
d. the Executive Order of 1965

_____ 9. The Act which prohibits the mandatory retirement of most employees under the age of 70 is

a. the Rehabilitation Act of 1973
b. the Civil Rights Act of 1964
c. the Age Discrimination in Employment Act of 1967
d. the Executive Order of 1965

_____10. An employee who sues his employer under a Worker's Compensation Act for injuries arising out of and in the course of his employment is subject to the defense of

a. contributory negligence
b. assumption of the risk
c. the fellow servant rule
d. none of the above

Short Essay

1. What is an agent's fiduciary duty?

2. What are the practical consequences of an agent's fiduciary duty?

3. What are the basic defenses available to an employer who has been charged with employment discrimination?

4. What are the remedies available to an employee who brings a successful employment discrimination action?

26

RELATIONSHIP WITH THIRD PARTIES

Chapter Outline

I. Relationship of Principal and Third Persons

   A. Contract Liability of the Principal

      1. Types of Authority
         a. Actual express authority
         b. Actual implied authority
         c. Apparent authority
      2. Delegation of Authority
      3. Effect of Termination of Agency Upon Authority
      4. Ratification

   B. Tort Liability of the Principal

      1. Direct Liability of Principal
      2. Vicarious Liability of Principal for Authorized Acts of Agent
      3. Vicarious Liability of Principal for Unauthorized Acts of Agent
         a. The doctrine of respondeat superior
         b. Torts of independent contractor

   C. Criminal Liability of the Principal

II. Relationship of Agent and Third Persons

   A. Contract Liability of Agent

      1. Unauthorized Contracts
         a. Agent's implied warranty of authority
         b. Misrepresentation

2. Undisclosed or Partially Disclosed Principal
    a. Liability of the parties
    b. Rights of undisclosed or partially disclosed principal
3. Liability of Agent Where Principal is Non-existent
4. Performance Guaranteed by Agent

B. Tort Liability of Agent

C. Rights of Agent Against Third Person

Definitions

1. Actual express authority
2. Actual implied authority
3. Apparent authority
4. Actual notice
5. Constructive notice
6. Ratification
7. Vicarious liability
8. Respondeat superior
9. Non-delegable duty
10. Implied warranty of authority
11. Undisclosed principal
12. Partially disclosed principal
13. Disclosed principal
14. Non-existent principal

True - False

_____ 1. An agent who has express authority to sell his principal's car ordinarily has implied authority to do whatever is reasonably necessary to sell the car.

_____ 2. An agent has no apparent authority to bind her principal in any transaction in which the identity of the principal is not disclosed.

_____ 3. An agent may not ordinarily appoint a subagent to perform the agent's duties.

_____ 4. An agent's actual authority is terminated by a revocation of authority.

_____ 5. An agent's apparent authority is terminated by a renunciation of authority.

_____ 6. A principal may not be held liable for the wrongful acts of his agent if the agent acted in flagrant disobedience of the principal's instructions.

_____ 7. Under the doctrine of respondeat superior, a principal may be held liable for the torts of her agent even though the agent is sufficiently solvent to pay for the damage himself.

_____ 8. A principal is ordinarily liable for the unauthorized criminal acts of his agents.

_____ 9. An agent who knowingly enters into a contract on behalf of a non-existent principal is personally liable on the contract.

_____ 10. An agent who is personally liable on a contract has no right of action against the third person for breach of the contract.

Multiple Choice

_____ 1. An agent may bind her principal by acts which are within the scope of her

a. express authority
b. implied authority
c. apparent authority
d. all of the above

_____ 2. An agent may be liable to his principal for exceeding his actual authority even though his acts are within the scope of his

a. express authority
b. implied authority
c. apparent authority
d. none of the above

_____ 3. An agent has apparent authority to bind her principal in any transaction in which

a. third persons have no knowledge of the agency relationship
b. the existence and identity of the principal are undisclosed
c. third persons reasonably rely upon the existence of actual authority as indicated by the principal's conduct
d. none of the above

_____ 4. When an agency is terminated by operation of law, the agent's apparent authority continues with respect to third parties with whom the agent had previously dealt until they

a. receive actual notice of the termination
b. receive constructive notice of the termination
c. read of the termination in a newspaper of general circulation
d. none of the above

_____ 5. An agent who, without authority, enters into a contract with a third person on behalf of his principal binds

a. his principal but not the third person
b. the third person but not his principal
c. neither his principal nor the third person
d. both his principal and the third person

_____ 6. Ratification of an unauthorized contract is effective to bind the principal and a third person to the contract even though

a. the principal does not ratify the entire contract
b. the principal does not notify the third person of his intent to ratify the contract
c. the third person has already notified the principal of his withdrawal from the contract
d. the agent failed to indicate to the third person that his acts were on behalf of the principal

_____ 7. If P directs his agent, A, to slash the tires on competitor C's car, who is liable to C for the damage?

a. P only
b. A only
c. both P and A
d. neither P nor A

_____ 8. The doctrine of respondeat superior imposes liability upon

a. an employer
b. an employee
c. an independent contractor
d. a fellow servant

_____ 9. Assume that A enters into a contract with T on behalf of A's undisclosed principal, P. If T fails to discover the existence of P, whom may T hold to performance of the contract?

a. A only
b. P only
c. A or P but not both
d. neither A nor P

_____ 10. Assume that A enters into a contract with T on behalf of A's undisclosed principal, P. If T discovers the existence and identity of P, whom may T hold to performance of the contract?

a. A only
b. P only
c. A or P but not both
d. neither A nor P

Short Essay

1. What is the difference between actual authority and apparent authority?

2. What is the difference between having the power to bind one's principal and having the right to bind him?

3. Under respondeat superior, who ultimately foots the bill for an employee's tortious conduct?

27

NATURE AND FORMATION

Chapter Outline

A. Nature of Partnership

1. Definition of Partnership
2. Entity Theory
   a. Partnership as a legal entity
   b. Partnership as a legal aggregate
3. Types of Partners

B. Formation of a Partnership

1. Association
   a. Articles of partnership
   b. Who may become partners
   c. Incidence of statute of frauds
   d. Firm name
2. Tests of Partnership Existence
   a. Business element
   b. Co-ownership
3. Partnership Capital

Definitions

1. Partnership

2. Person

3. Legal entity

4. Aggregate

5. General partner

6. Limited partner

7. Silent partner

8. Secret partner

9. Dormant partner

10. Articles of partnership

11. Joint venture

12. Capital contribution

13. Partnership capital

14. Partnership property

True - False

_____ 1. Every partner is considered an agent of the partnership.

_____ 2. Any one partner may be held liable for the entire indebtedness of the partnership.

_____ 3. A partnership is required to pay Federal income tax on its income.

_____ 4. A partnership agreement must be in writing.

_____ 5. A partnership may use the name of an existing corporation as long as no other partnership is using that name.

_____ 6. A person may be a partner even though he has no authority to conduct the ordinary activities of the business.

_____ 7. A partnership relation exists whenever a person has any right to manage and control the business.

_____ 8. A partner may not ordinarily withdraw his capital contribution without the consent of all the partners.

_____ 9. Upon dissolution, a debt owing to a partner has priority over debts owing to creditors.

_____ 10. Partners may agree to share the profits and losses of the business unequally.

Multiple Choice

_____ 1. Under the U.P.A., a partnership may be formed by two or more

a. individuals
b. partnerships
c. corporations
d. all of the above

_____ 2. A general partner is one

a. who is liable for partnership indebtedness only to the extent of the capital which he has contributed
b. who has full management power
c. whose membership in the firm is disclosed to the public
d. none of the above

_____ 3. No person may become the member of a partnership without the consent of

a. at least one partner
b. two or more partners
c. a majority of the partners
d. all of the partners

_____ 4. A partnership agreement entered into by an adjudicated incompetent is

a. void
b. voidable
c. unenforceable
d. none of the above

_____ 5. A minor partner who disaffirms the partnership agreement is personally liable to partnership creditors to the extent of

a. his capital contribution
b. his accrued and unpaid share of the profits
c. the entire indebtedness of the partnership
d. (a) and (b) but not (c)

_____ 6. No writing is required in order to enforce

a. a contract for the transfer of interest in land to or by a partnership
b. a contract to form a partnership for a period longer than one year
c. the promise of an incoming partner to assume existing debts incurred in the prior operations of the business
d. all of the above

_____ 7. The name of a partnership should <u>not</u> be

a. a fictitious or assumed name
b. deceptively similar to the name of any other existing business concern
c. the name of only one of the partners
d. all of the above

_____ 8. A partnership agreement which restricts the authority of particular partners to bind the partnership is

a. void
b. voidable
c. unenforceable
d. none of the above

_____ 9. A person who is entitled to receive a share of the profits of a partnership is prima facie a partner unless the payment is of

a. a debt to a creditor
b. rent to a landlord
c. wages to an employee
d. all of the above

_____10. Title to real estate which is purchased with partnership funds may stand in the name of

a. the partnership
b. an individual partner
c. a third party
d. all of the above

Short Essay

1. What are the factors considered by a court in determining whether a partnership relation exists?

2. Why would anyone want to prove the existence of a partnership relation?

3. Is a partnership a legal entity? Explain.

28

RIGHTS AND DUTIES

Chapter Outline

I. Relationships of Partners to One Another

A. Duties Among Partners

1. Fiduciary Duty
2. Duty of Obedience
3. Duty of Care

B. Rights Among Partners

1. Rights in Specific Partnership Property
2. Partner's Interest in the Partnership
   a. Assignability
   b. Creditors' rights
3. Right to Distributions
   a. Right to share in profits
   b. Right to return of capital
   c. Right to compensation

4. Right to Participate in Management
5. Right to Choose Associates
6. Enforcement Rights
   a. Right to information and inspection of the books
   b. Right to an accounting

II. Relationship Between Partners and Third Parties

A. Contracts of Partnership

1. Contract Liability of Partners

2. Authority to Bind Partnership
    a. Actual express authority
    b. Actual implied authority
    c. Apparent authority
3. Partnership by Estoppel

B. Torts of Partnership

C. Admissions of and Notice to a Partner

D. Liability of Incoming Partner

Definitions

1. Partner's interest in partnership

2. Tenancy in partnership

3. Charging order

4. Delectus personae

5. Actual express authority

6. Actual implied authority

7. Apparent authority

8. Partnership by estoppel

9. Vicarious liability

10. Joint liability

11. Several liability

12. Accounting

True - False

_____ 1. A partner may not ordinarily use partnership property for his own purposes.

_____ 2. A partner who fails to use ordinary care and skill in discharging his assigned duties will be personally liable to his partners for any resulting loss.

_____ 3. A partner's interest in specific partnership property is not subject to attachment by his individual creditors.

_____ 4. A partner who sells his interest in the partnership remains a patrtner with all the usual rights and duties.

_____ 5. A partner's interest in the partnership is not subject to the claims of his individual creditors.

_____ 6. Unless otherwise agreed, partners bear losses in the same proportion in which they share profits.

_____ 7. A partner who performs a disproportionate share of the partnership duties is entitled to a salary in addition to his share of the profits.

_____ 8. A partner may not ordinarily inspect the books of the partnership after business hours.

_____ 9. The majority generally governs the actions and decisions of the partnership.

_____10. A partner who commits a tort in the ordinary course of the business of the partnership must indemnify the partnership for any damages it pays to the third party.

Multiple Choice

_____ 1. The rights and duties of the partners among themselves are determined by

a. the partnership agreement
b. the common law
c. the Uniform Partnership Act
d. all of the above

_____ 2. The rights and duties of the partners with respect to the third persons with whom the partnership deals are determined by

a. the partnership agreement
b. the Uniform Third Persons Act
c. the Uniform Partnership Act
d. none of the above

_____ 3. A partner may make an individual assignment of

a. his rights in specific partnership property
b. his share of the profits of the partnership
c. his right to participate in the assets upon liquidation of the partnership
d. (b) and (c) but not (a)

_____ 4. A person who is entitled to participate in the management of a partnership is generally

a. an individual partner's assignee
b. an individual partner's judgment creditor
c. a receiver for an individual partner's interest
d. none of the above

_____ 5. A partner is entitled to receive interest on

a. his capital contributions to the partnership
b. his advancements to the partnership over and above his agreed capital contributions
c. both of the above
d. neither of the above

_____ 6. A partner may bind the partnership by an act which is <u>not</u> apparently within the scope of the partnership business if he has

a. express authority to perform the act
b. implied authority to perform the act
c. either (a) or (b)
d. neither (a) nor (b)

_____ 7. A partner who has actual authority from a majority of his co-partners may bind the partnership to

a. an assignment of partnership property for the benefit of its creditors
b. a sale of partnership property held for sale in the usual course of business
c. a sale of partnership property not held for sale in the usual course of business
d. a contract of suretyship in the firm name

_____ 8. The liability of an incoming partner upon antecedent debts and obligations of the firm is

a. unlimited
b. limited to his capital contribution
c. limited to his accrued and unpaid share of the profits
d. none of the above

_____ 9. The books of the partnership may be

a. kept at the home of one of the partners
b. inspected by the legal representative of a deceased partner at any time
c. inspected by any certified accountant on behalf of a creditor
d. none of the above

_____ 10. An action for an accounting may be brought

a. at law
b. in equity
c. at law or in equity
d. none of the above

Short Essay

1. What standard is applied to determine whether partners may by agreement vary their legal rights and obligations?

2. List five specific instances in which partners may by agreement vary their legal rights and obligations.

3. List six specific instances in which a partner may have actual implied authority to bind the partnership.

29

DISSOLUTION AND TERMINATION

Chapter Outline

A. Dissolution

1. Causes of Dissolution
   a. Dissolution by act of the parties
   b. Dissolution by operation of law
   c. Dissolution by court order
2. Effects of Dissolution
   a. On authority
   b. On existing liability

B. Winding Up

1. The Right to Wind Up
2. Distribution of Assets
   a. Solvent partnership
   b. Insolvent partnership
   c. Contribution of partner upon insolvency
3. Marshalling of assets

C. Continuation of Partnership After Dissolution

1. Partners' Right to Continue Partnership
   a. Continuation after wrongful dissolution
   b. Continuation after expulsion
   c. Continuation per agreement of the parties
2. Rights of Creditors

Definitions

1. Dissolution

2. Winding up

3. Liquidation

4. Termination

5. Rightful dissolution

6. Actual notice

7. Constructive notice

8. Solvent partnership

9. Insolvent partnership

10. Marshalling of assets

11. Continuation

12. Wrongful dissolution

13. Continuation agreement

True - False

_____ 1. A partnership is dissolved whenever it undergoes any change in membership.

_____ 2. A partner always has the power to dissolve the partnership.

_____ 3. A partner who withdraws in violation of the partnership agreement remains a partner with all the usual rights and duties.

_____ 4. Dissolution terminates the actual authority of a partner to complete existing contracts.

_____ 5. Dissolution discharges the existing liability of each partner.

_____ 6. A retiring partner will be discharged from his existing liabilities by entering into a novation with the continuing partners.

_____ 7. The proportion in which the partners bear losses depends upon their relative capital contributions.

_____ 8. A partnership is liable for the personal obligations of its partners.

_____ 9. A partner who wrongfully withdraws from the partnership is liable to the remaining partners for damages resulting from the breach of the partnership agreement.

_____10. A retiring partner is ordinarily entitled to be paid the value of his interest as of the date of the dissolution.

_____11. A retiring partner may be liable upon contracts which are entered into by the partnership subsequent to his withdrawal.

Multiple Choice

_____ 1. Dissolution is brought about by

a. the assignment of a partner's interest
b. the bankruptcy of a partner
c. a creditor's charging order on a partner's interest
d. all of the above

_____ 2. Dissolution will not be brought about by

a. the death of a partner
b. the bankruptcy of the partnership
c. an action for an accounting
d. a withdrawal in violation of the partnership agreement

_____ 3. A court will order a dissolution if it finds that

a. a partner is insane
b. a partner has breached the partnership agreement
c. the business has been losing money
d. all of the above

_____ 4. Assume A, B, and C form a partnership to erect an office building. If A assigns his interest to T, T may petition the court to dissolve the partnership

a. at any time
b. as soon as partnership liabilities exceed partnership assets
c. as soon as the building is completed
d. none of the above

_____ 5. Apparent authority is not sufficient to bind the partnership after dissolution if

a. the third party extended credit to the partnership prior to dissolution
b. the third party never extended credit to the partnership prior to dissolution but nevertheless knew of the partnership
c. the third party never extended credit to the partnership prior to dissolution nor knew of the partnership
d. (b) and (c) but not (a)

_____ 6. A partner cannot force the liquidation of the partnership if

a. he has wrongfully dissolved the partnership
b. he has been expelled pursuant to the partnership agreement
c. the partnership agreement provides for the continuation of the partnership
d. all of the above

_____ 7. In a liquidation of a general partnership, the last items to be paid are amounts owing

a. to partners in respect of profits
b. to partners in respect of capital
c. to partners other than for capital and profits
d. to creditors who are not also partners

_____ 8. Assume that A, B, and C form a partnership with A contributing $1,000 capital, B contributing $5,000 capital, and C contributing $10,000 capital. Each partner has also loaned the partnership $2,000 which has not been repaid. When the partnership is liquidated, its assets are $50,000 and its liabilities to creditors are $25,000. How much will A receive?

a. $1,000
b. $2,000
c. $4,000
d. none of the above

_____ 9. Assume that A, B, and C form a partnership with A contributing $2,000 capital, B contributing $10,000 capital, and C contributing $16,000 capital. Each partner has also loaned the partnership $2,000 which has not been repaid. When the partnership is liquidated, its assets are $50,000 and its liabilities to creditors are $25,000. How much will B receive?

a. $4,000
b. $8,000
c. $12,000
d. none of the above

_____10. Assume that A, B, and C form a partnership with A contributing $6,000 capital, B contributing $10,000 capital, and C contributing $14,000 capital. Each partner has also loaned the partnership $5,000 which has not been repaid. When the partnership is liquidated, its asset are $50,000, its liabilities to creditors are $50,000, and A is insolvent. How much will C receive?

a. $1,000
b. $2,000
c. $4,000
d. none of the above

Short Essay

1. What steps are usually taken in winding up the affairs of a partnership?

2. What are the three major causes of dissolution?

3. What is the order of distribution of an insolvent partner's assets under the U.P.A.?

4. What is the order of distribution of a general partnership's assets?

30

LIMITED PARTNERSHIPS

Chapter Outline

A. Limited Partnerships

1. Definition
2. Formation
    a. Filing of certificate
    b. Name
    c. Contributions
    d. Defective formation
    e. Foreign limited partnerships
3. Rights
    a. Control
    b. Assignment of interest
    c. Profit sharing
    d. Return of contribution
    e. Loans
4. Duties and liabilities
    a. Duties
    b. Liabilities
5. Dissolution
    a. Causes
    b. Distribution of assets

B. Other Types of Unincorporated Business Associations

1. Joint Venture
2. Joint Stock Company
3. Mining Partnerships
4. Limited Partnership Associations
5. Business Trusts
6. Unincorporated Associations

Definitions

1. Limited partnership

2. Equity participant

3. Foreign limited partnership

4. Substituted limited partner

5. Certificate of limited partnership

6. Joint stock company

7. Joint venture

8. Mining partnership

9. Limited partnership association

10. Business trust

11. Unincorporated association

True - False

_____ 1. The liability of a limited partner for partnership debts or obligations is usually limited to his capital contibution.

_____ 2. Under the R.U.L.P.A., a certificate of limited partnership must be filed in the office of the Attorney General of the State in which the limited partnership has its principal office.

_____ 3. A limited partner is liable to the partnership for the difference between what he has actually contributed and what he agreed to contribute.

_____ 4. An equity participant who erroneously believes that he has become a limited partner in a limited partnership will be liable as a general partner to any third party who transacts business with the enterprise.

_____ 5. A general partner of a limited partnership has all the rights of a partner in a partnership without limited partners.

_____ 6. A limited partner may not assign his interest without the consent of all of the partners.

_____ 7. Unless otherwise agreed, under the R.U.L.P.A. the profits of a limited partnership are allocated on the basis of the value of contributions actually made by each partner.

_____ 8. A limited partner owes a fiduciary duty to his general partners.

_____ 9. A general partner owes a ficuciary duty to his limited partners.

_____10. The liability of a general partner in a limited partnership for partnership debts or obligations is limited to his capital contribution.

_____11. A limited partner has the same power to dissolve the partnership that a general partner has.

Multiple Choice

_____ 1. A limited partnership may be composed of

a. one general partner and one limited partner
b. two limited partners
c. one general partner and two limited partners
d. (a) and (c) but not (b)

_____ 2. The names of all limited partners should be included in

a. the certificate of limited partnership
b. the name of the partnership
c. each partner's income tax return
d. all of the above

_____ 3. Under the U.L.P.A., the capital contribution of a limited partner may not be made in

a. cash
b. services
c. real property
d. personal property

_____ 4. Under the R.U.L.P.A., if a limited partnership transacts business in a foreign State without first registering to transact business in that State

a. its limited partners will be liable as general partners in the foreign State's courts
b. it may not defend itself in the foreign State's courts
c. it may not bring enforcement actions in the foreign State's courts
d. (b) and (c) but not (a)

_____ 5. Under the R.U.L.P.A., a limited partner forfeits his limited liability if he

a. becomes an agent of the limited partnership
b. advises a general partner with respect to the business of the limited partnership
c. votes on a change in the nature of the business
d. none of the above

_____ 6. If a limited partner makes a loan to the partnership, he is entitled to repayment of the loan

a. before general creditors of the partnership are repaid
b. on a pro rata basis with general creditors of the partnership
c. after general creditors of the partnership are repaid
d. none of the above

_____ 7. A limited partnership is dissolved upon

a. the death of a limited partner
b. the bankruptcy of a limited partner
c. the withdrawal of a general partner
d. all of the above

_____ 8. Under the R.U.L.P.A., unless otherwise agreed, a limited partner is entitled to repayment of his capital contribution

a. before general partners are repaid their capital contributions
b. on a pro rata basis with general partners
c. after general partners are repaid theri capital contributions
d. none of the above

_____ 9. Which of the following unincorporated business associations is dissolved by the death of a member?

a. a joint stock company
b. a mining partnership
c. a limited partnership association
d. none of the above

_____10. Which of the following unincorporated business associations may be formed without the authorization or consent of the state?

a. a joint stock company
b. a business trust
c. a joint venture
d. all of the above

Short Essay

1. When may a limited partner rightfully demand the return of his contributions?

2. When may a limited partner be subject to unlimited personal liability for the debts and obligations of the partnership?

3. According to the R.U.L.P.A., when may a limited partnership be dissolved?

4. What are the duties owed by a general partner to the limited partnership?

31

NATURE AND FORMATION

Chapter Outline

I. Nature of Corporations

   A. Corporate Attributes

      1. Legal Entity
      2. Creature of the State
      3. Limited Liability
      4. Free Transferability of Corporate Shares
      5. Perpetual Existence
      6. Centralized Management
      7. As a Person
      8. As a Citizen

   B. Classification of Corporations

      1. Public or Private
      2. Profit or Non-profit
      3. Domestic or Foreign
      4. Closely Held
      5. Professional Corporations

II. Formation of a Corporation

   A. Organizing the Corporation

      1. Promoters
         a. Promoters' contracts
         b. Promoters' fiduciary duty
      2. Subscribers
      3. Selection of State for Incorporation

B. Formalities of Incorporation

1. Selection of Name
2. Incorporators
3. Articles of Incorporation
4. Organization Meeting
5. By-laws

III. Recognition and Disregard of Corporateness

A. Recognition of Corporateness

1. Corporation de Jure
2. Corporation de Facto
3. Corporation by Estoppel
4. Defective Corporation

B. Disregard of Corporateness

1. Closely Held Corporations
2. Parent-Subsidiary

IV. Corporate Powers

A. Sources of Corporate Powers

1. Statutory Powers
2. Express Charter Powers
3. Implied Powers

B. Ultra Vires Acts

1. Effect of Ultra Vires Acts
2. Remedies for Ultra Vires Acts

C. Liability for Torts and Crimes

Definitions

1. Corporation
2. Management
3. Public corporation
4. Private corporation
5. Profit corporation
6. Non-profit corporation
7. Domestic corporation
8. Foreign corporation
9. Closely-held corporation
10. Professional corporation
11. Promoter
12. Subscriber
13. Articles of incorporation
14. Incorporators
15. By-laws
16. Corporation de jure
17. Corporation de facto
18. Corporation by estoppel
19. Defective corporation
20. Piercing the corporate veil
21. Ultra vires

True - False

_____ 1. Shareholders are personally liable for the corporation's debts up to the amount of their investment.

_____ 2. A corporation is liable for the personal obligations of its shareholders.

_____ 3. A shareholder is neither a principal nor an agent of the corporation.

_____ 4. A non-profit corporation may make a profit.

_____ 5. A promoter who enters into a pre-incorporation contract in the name of the corporation is ordinarily personally liable on that contract.

_____ 6. Under the M.B.C.A., a subscription may be revoked at any time prior to its acceptance.

_____ 7. A corporation must be incorporated in the State in which it has its principal place of business.

_____ 8. The by-laws of a corporation may not be changed without shareholder approval.

_____ 9. A corporation may be created by estoppel.

_____10. Under the M.B.C.A.,persons who assume to act as a corporation without authority to do so are subject to unlimited personal liability for the debts of the enterprise.

_____11. A general statement of corporate purpose is sufficient to give rise to all of the powers necessary to accomplish that purpose.

_____12. A corporation is liable for the torts and crimes committed by its agents in the course of their employment.

Multiple Choice

_____ 1. A corporation

a. may sue or be sued by one of its shareholders
b. is dissolved by a transfer of its stock from one individual to another
c. may not own or deal in real property
d. all of the above

_____ 2. A corporation is dissolved by

a. the death of a director
b. the withdrawal of an officer
c. the bankruptcy of a shareholder
d. none of the above

_____ 3. The officers of a corporation

a. must be shareholders of the corporation
b. are elected by the shareholders of the corporation
c. are appointed by the board of directors of the corporation
d. (a) and (c) but not (b)

_____ 4. If a corporation transacts business in a foreign State without first qualifying to transact business in that State

a. its contracts are invalid in the foreign State's courts
b. it may not defend itself in the foreign State's courts
c. it may not bring enforcement actions in the foreign State's courts
d. (b) and (c) but not (a)

_____ 5. A corporation becomes liable on a preincorporation contract made by promoters in the name of the corporation and in its behalf when

a. the contract is executed
b. the corporation is formed
c. the corporation adopts or ratifies the contract
d. none of the above

_____ 6. The promoters of a corporation owe a ficuciary duty to

a. each other
b. subscribers
c. initial shareholders
d. all of the above

_____ 7. The existence of a de facto corporation can be challenged by

a. the state
b. creditors of the corporation
c. debtors of the corporation
d. none of the above

_____ 8. Piercing the corporate veil

a. invalidates the contracts of the corporation
b. imposes personal liability upon the shareholders for the obligations of the corporation
c. denies the corporation access to the state's courts
d. (b) and (c) but not (a)

_____ 9. Under the M.B.C.A., a corporation may

a. lend money to its employees
b. be a shareholder in other corporations
c. make charitable contributions
d. all of the above

_____ 10. Under the M.B.C.A., the defense of ultra vires in an action for breach of contract by or against a corporation

a. is unavailable
b. is available where the contract is wholly executory on both sides
c. is available where the corporation has received full performance from the other party
d. is available where the other party has received full performance from the corporation

_____ 11. A corporation

a. is not capable of committing a crime
b. is capable of committing a crime but may not be punished by imprisonment
c. is capable of committing a crime but may not be punished by fine
d. none of the above

Short Essay

1. What distinguishes a corporation from a partnership?

2. Under what conditions may a de facto corporation be formed?

3. When is a court likely to pierce the corporate veil?

32

FINANCIAL STRUCTURE

Chapter Outline

I. Debt Securities

  A. Authority to Issue Debt Securities

  B. Types of Debt Securities

    1. Unsecured Bonds
    2. Secured Bonds
    3. Income Bonds
    4. Convertible Bonds
    5. Callable Bonds

II. Equity Securities

  A. Issuance of Shares

    1. Authority to Issue
    2. Qualification of Stock
    3. Pre-emptive Rights
    4. Amount of Consideration for Shares
       a. Par value stock
       b. No par value stock
       c. Treasury stock
    5. Payment for Newly Issued Shares
       a. Type of consideration
       b. Valuation of consideration
    6. Liability for Shares

B. Classes of Shares

1. Common Stock
2. Preferred Stock
   a. Dividend preferences
   b. Liquidation preferences
   c. Additional rights and limitations

III. Dividends and Other Distributions

A. Types of Dividends and Other Distributions

1. Cash Dividends
2. Property Dividends
3. Stock Dividends
4. Stock Splits
5. Liquidating Dividends
6. Redemption of Shares
7. Acquisition of Shares

B. Legal Restrictions on Dividends and Other Distributions

1. Definitions
2. Legal Restrictions on Cash Dividends
   a. Earned surplus test
   b. Surplus test
   c. Amended MBCA test
   d. Nimble dividends
3. Legal Restrictions on Liquidating Distributions
4. Legal Restrictions on Redemptions and Acquisition of Shares

C. Declaration and Payment of Dividends

D. Liability for Improper Dividends and Distributions

IV. Transfer of Investment Securities

A. Ownership of Securities

1. Record Ownership
2. Duty of Issuer to Register Transfer of Security
3. Lost, Destroyed, or Stolen Certificated Securities

B. Transfer of Securities

1. Manner of Transfer
2. Bona Fide Purchasers
3. Transfer Warranties
4. Forged or Unauthorized Indorsement

Definitions

1. Equity security
2. Debt security
3. Pre-emptive right
4. Par value stock
5. Stated capital
6. Capital surplus
7. No par value stock
8. Treasury stock
9. Common stock
10. Preferred stock
11. Cumulative dividend
12. Non-cumulative dividend
13. Liquidating dividend
14. Insolvency test
15. Nimble dividends
16. Earned surplus
17. Surplus
18. Net assets
19. Earned surplus test
20. Surplus test
21. Amended MBCA test
22. Uncertificated security
23. Certificated security

True - False

_____ 1. Equity securities create a debtor-creditor relationship between the corporation and the shareholder.

_____ 2. The board of directors of a corporation may not issue bonds or other obligations in the name of the corporation without shareholder approval.

_____ 3. The amount of shares that a corporation is authorized to issue may not be changed without shareholder approval.

_____ 4. Shares without par value may be issued for any amount set by the board of directors.

_____ 5. The rights of preferred shareholders are subordinate to the rights of all of the creditors of the corporation.

_____ 6. No dividend is payable upon any class of stock unless duly declared by the board of directors.

_____ 7. Shares of common stock are frequently redeemable by the corporation at a call price stated in the stock certificate.

_____ 8. A corporation may not pay a dividend when the payment of the dividend would render the corporation insolvent.

_____ 9. Under the MBCA, a corporation may purchase its own shares only out of earned surplus.

_____ 10. Once properly declared, a cash dividend is considered a debt owing by the corporation to the shareholders.

_____ 11. In most states, an unsuspecting shareholder who receives an illegal dividend from an insolvent corporation cannot be compelled to make a refund.

_____ 12. Title to a certificated security cannot be transferred through a forged or unauthorized indorsement.

Multiple Choice

_____ 1. The claim of a secured creditor is enforceable

a. only against the general assets of the corporation
b. only against specific property of the corporation
c. against both the general assets and specific property of the corporation
d. none of the above

_____ 2. A corporation that sells its shares of stock in violation of the applicable regulatory statutes is subject to

a. court injunction
b. possible criminal prosecution
c. civil liability in damages
d. all of the above

_____ 3. The par value of a share of stock must

a. be stated in the articles of incorporation
b. reflect the actual value of the share
c. reflect the actual price paid to the corporation
d. (b) and (c) but not (a)

_____ 4. Treasury shares may be

a. voted
b. paid dividends
c. sold at less than par value
d. none of the above

_____ 5. Valid consideration for the issuance of capital stock includes

a. promissory notes
b. real property
c. future services
d. all of the above

_____ 6. Shares of stock which are redeemed by the corporation become

a. unauthorized shares
b. authorized but unissued shares
c. issued but not outstanding shares
d. treasury shares

_____ 7. Capital surplus may result from

a. an allocation of part of the consideration received for no-par shares
b. any consideration in excess of par value received for par shares
c. a reappraisal upward of certain corporate assets
d. all of the above

_____ 8. A shareholder may maintain an action at law against the corporation to recover a dividend whenever

a. unreserved and unrestricted earned surplus is available for payment of the dividend
b. the dividend may be paid out of capital surplus without impairing stated capital
c. the dividend has been formally declared by resolution of the board of directors
d. all of the above

_____ 9. A stock dividend

a. may be revoked unless actually distributed
b. cannot be rescinded as against non-assenting shareholders
c. is considered a debt owing by the corporation to the shareholders
d. (b) and (c) but not (a)

_____10. A purchaser for value and without notice of adverse claims who receives a reregistered certificated security on registration of transfer warrants that

a. the transfer is effective and rightful
b. he has no knowledge of any unauthorized signature in a necessary indorsement
c. the security has not been materially altered
d. all of the above

_____11. An issuer who registers the transfer of a certificated security upon an unauthorized indorsement is subject to liability for

a. conversion
b. interference with contractual relations
c. improper registration
d. fraudulent misrepresentation

Short Essay

1. What are the rights of a shareholder?

2. Why is preferred stock usually issued with a par value?

3. When will a court of equity grant an injunction requiring the directors of a corporation to declare a dividend?

4. What warranties are given by a person who transfers certificated securities to a purchaser for value?

33

MANAGEMENT STRUCTURE

Chapter Outline

I. Role of Shareholders

  A. Voting Rights of Shareholders

    1. Election and Removal of Directors
    2. Approval of Fundamental Changes
    3. Concentrations of Voting Power
       a. Proxies
       b. Voting trusts
       c. Shareholder agreements

  B. Enforcement Rights of Shareholders

    1. Right to Inspect Books and Records
    2. Shareholder Suits
       a. Direct suits
       b. Derivative suits
    3. Shareholder's Right to Dissent

  C. Liability of Shareholders

    1. Defective Incorporation
    2. Disregard of the Corporate Entity
    3. Illegal Distributions
    4. Controlling Shareholders

II. Role of Directors and Officers

  A. Function of the Board of Directors
    1. Selection and Removal of Officers
    2. Capital Structure
    3. Fundamental Changes

4. Dividends
5. Management Compensation

B. Qualification, Election, and Tenure of Directors

1. Qualification of Directors
2. Election, Number and Tenure of Directors
3. Vacancies and Removal of Directors
4. Compensation of Directors

C. Exercise of Directors' Functions

1. Meetings
2. Quorum
3. Action Taken Without a Meeting
4. Delegation of Board Powers
5. Directors' Inspection Rights

D. Officers

1. Selection and Removal of Officers
2. Role of Officers
    a. President
    b. Vice-president
    c. Secretary
    d. Treasurer
3. Authority of Officers
    a. Actual express authority
    b. Actual implied authority
    c. Apparent authority
    d. Ratification

E. Duties of Directors and Officers

1. Duty of Obedience
2. Duty of Diligence
    a. Reliance Upon Others
    b. Business Judgment Rule
3. Duty of Loyalty
    a. Conflict of interests
    b. Corporate opportunity
    c. Transactions in shares
    d. Duty not to compete

F. Liabilities of Directors and Officers

1. Breach of Duties to Corporation
2. Defective Incorporation
3. Contracts
4. Torts
5. Violation of State and Federal Statutes
6. Illegal Distributions

Definitions

1. Pyramidal management structure

2. Quorum

3. Classification of directors

4. Cumulative voting

5. Proxy

6. Voting trust

7. Shareholder agreement

8. Direct suit

9. Derivative suit

10. Right to dissent

11. Controlling shareholder

12. Fundamental change

13. Business judgment rule

14. Corporate opportunity

True - False

_____ 1. A corporation may not issue non-voting stock.

_____ 2. A shareholder normally has one vote for each share owned.

_____ 3. Shareholders may not remove any director without just cause.

_____ 4. Any recovery in a shareholder's direct suit usually goes to the corporate treasury so that all shareholders can benefit proportionately.

_____ 5. A shareholder may not may not bring a derivative suit without first making demand upon the board of directors to enforce the corporate right.

_____ 6. A shareholder who has not fully paid the required consideration for his shares is liable for the deficiency.

_____ 7. Once established, the number of directors may not be increased or decreased.

_____ 8. Under the MBCA, each director is entitled to fix his own compensation.

_____ 9. Directors do not have the power to bind the corporation when acting individually.

_____ 10. Directors may not vote by proxy.

_____ 11. Officers may be removed by the board with or without cause.

_____ 12. Whenever an officer breaches his ficuciary duty he forfeits his right to compensation during the period he engaged in the breach.

Multiple Choice

_____ 1. Special shareholder meetings may be called by

a. any member of the board of directors
b. any shareholder
c. any person so authorized in the articles of incorporation
d. all of the above

_____ 2. The board of directors may be classified into

a. three groups
b. six groups
c. nine groups
d. none of the above

_____ 3. Assume that X corporation has two shareholders, A and B, and 100 shares of voting stock. If X corporation uses cumulative voting, how many shares would A need to elect three of the five directors?

a. 50
b. 51
c. 60
d. 61

_____ 4. In gneral, a proxy

a. must be in writing to be effective
b. is not revocable unless coupled with an interest
c. transfers legal title to the stock
d. (a) and (b) but not (c)

_____ 5. Which of the following are agents of the corporation?

a. shareholders
b. directors
c. officers
d. (b) and (c) but not (a)

_____ 6. Under the modern view, the board of directors must consist of at least

a. one member
b. three members
c. nine members
d. none of the above

_____ 7. Assume that X corporation has nine directors. What is the minimum number of directors that may bind the corporation?

a. one
b. three
c. five
d. nine

_____ 8. An executive committee may be appointed by the board to

a. amend the by-laws
b. authorize the sale of stock
c. declare dividends
d. set management compensation

_____ 9. The same person may <u>not</u> simultaneously hold the office of

a. president and vice-president
b. president and secretary
c. president and treasurer
d. secretary and treasurer

_____10. A contract between a director and the corporation is neither void nor voidable, if

a. it is approved after full disclosure by the board of disinterested directors
b. it is fair and reasonable to the corporation
c. either (a) or (b)
d. neither (a) nor (b)

_____11. A director can take personal advantage of an opportunity

a. in which the corporation has a property interest
b. which the corporation is financially unable to accept
c. which the corporation expressly accepts by a vote of disinterested directors after full disclosure
d. none of the above

Short Essay

1. When may a shareholder be denied his right to inspect the books and records of the corporation?

2. List five actions that may be initiated by the board of directors but require shareholder approval.

3. List four actions that may be taken by the board of directors without shareholder approval.

4. What are the duties of directors and officers?

5. What is the standard of care imposed upon directors and officers?

34

FUNDAMENTAL CHANGES

Chapter Outline

A. Charter Amendments

B. Combinations

1. Purchase or Lease of All or Substantially All of the Assets
2. Purchase of Shares
3. Compulsory Share Exchange
4. Merger
5. Consolidation
6. Dissenting Shareholders

C. Dissolution

1. Nonjudicial Dissolution
2. Judicial Dissolution
3. Liquidation
4. Protection of Creditors

Definitions

1. Fundamental change

2. Appraisal remedy

3. Articles of amendment

4. Combination

5. Merger

6. Surviving corporation

7. Consolidation

9. Dissenting shareholder

10. Fair value

11. Nonjudicial dissolution

12. Involuntary judicial dissolution

13. Liquidation

14. Compulsory Share Exchange

True - False

_____ 1. Changes which alter the basic structure of the corporation require shareholder approval

_____ 2. Shareholder approval for fundamental changes must be unanimous.

_____ 3. Under the MBCA, shareholders who dissent from some charter amendments are accorded the right to recover from the corporation the fair value of their shares.

_____ 4. Charter amendments do not affect the existing rights of non-shareholders.

_____ 5. All debts and other liabilities of a merged corporation are assumed by the surviving corporation.

_____ 6. In a consolidation of two or more corporations, each of the constituent corporations ceases to exist.

_____ 7. Nonjudicial dissolution may be brought about by voluntary action on the part of the holders of a majority of the outstanding shares of stock.

_____ 8. Involuntary dissolution by judicial proceeding may be instituted by the creditors of the corporation.

_____ 9. A corporation is subject to involuntary judicial dissolution if the shareholders are deadlocked and cannot elect directors.

_____ 10. When liquidation is involunatary, it is carried out by a court-appointed receiver.

_____ 11. When liquidation is voluntary, it is carried out by the board of directors.

_____ 12. Under a compulsory share exchange approval of the shareholders of the acquiring corporation is required.

Multiple Choice

_____ 1. Under the M.B.C.A., a corporation may amend its charter to

a. change its corporate name
b. change the preferential rights of shares
c. deny preemptive rights
d. all of the above

_____ 2. Charter amendments become effective upon

a. adopton of a resolution by the board setting forth the proposed amendment
b. approval by a majority vote of the shareholders
c. execution and filing of articles of amendment with the Secretary of State
d. issuance of the certificate of amendment by the Secretary of State

_____ 3. A corporation ceases to exist as a separate entity when

a. all or substantially all of its assets are purchased by another corporation
b. a controlling interest in its stock is purchased by another corporation
c. it is merged into another corporation
d. all of the above

_____ 4. The sale or lease of all or substantially all of a corporation's assets in the usual course of its business requires approval by its

a. board of directors
b. shareholders
c. board of directors and shareholders
d. none of the above

_____ 5. A corporation ceases to exist as a separate entity when

a. it purchases all or substantially all of the assets of another corporation
b. it purchases a controlling interest in the stock of another corporation
c. another corporation is merged into it
d. none of the above

_____ 6. The sale or lease of all or substantially all of a corporation's assets not in the usual course of its business requires approval by its

a. board of directors
b. shareholders
c. board of directors and shareholders
d. none of the above

_____ 7. A merger requires the approval of

a. the board of directors of each corporation
b. the board of directors and shareholders of each corporation
c. the board of directors and shareholders of the merged corporation
d. the shareholders of each corporation

_____ 8. The merger of a wholly-owned subsidiary into its parent requires the approval of

a. the board of directors of the parent corporation
b. the board of directors and shareholders of the subsidiary corporation
c. the board of directors and shareholders of each corporation
d. the shareholders of the subsidiary corporation

_____ 9. If a wholly-owned subsidiary is merged into its parent, an appraisal remedy is available to the shareholders of

a. the parent corporation
b. the subsidiary corporation
c. both the parent and the subsidiary
d. none of the above

_____ 10. A consolidation requires the approval of

a. the board of directors of each constituent corporation
b. the shareholders of each constituent corporation
c. the board of directors and shareholders of each constituent corporation
d. none of the above

_____ 11. The corporation may pay dissenting shareholders out of

a. earned surplus
b. capital surplus
c. stated capital
d. all of the above

Short Essay

1. List five examples of fundamental changes.

2. Outline the procedure for amending the articles of incorporation.

3. By what methods may a corporation acquire all or substantially all of the assets of another corporation?

4. What must a dissenting shareholder do to perfect his right to payment for his shares?

35

Secured Transactions and Suretyship

Chapter Outline

I. Secured Transactions in Personal Property

   A. Classification of Collateral

      1. Goods
         a. Consumer goods
         b. Equipment
         c. Farm products
         d. Inventory
         e. Fixtures
      2. Indispensable Paper
         a. Chattle paper
         b. Instruments
         c. Documents
      3. Intangibles
         a. Accounts
         b. General intangibles

   B. Attachment

      1. Value
      2. Debtor's Rights in Collateral
      3. Security Agreement
         a. After-acquired property
         b. Future advances

   C. Perfection

      1. Filing a Financing Statement
         a. Where to file

b. Improper filing
c. Subsequent change of information
2. Possession
3. Automatic Perfection
a. Purchase money security interest in consumer goods
b. Temporary perfection

D. Priorities

1. Against Unsecured Creditors
2. Against Lien Creditors
3. Against Other Secured Creditors
a. Perfected versus unperfected
b. Perfected versus perfected
c. Unperfected versus unperfected
4. Against Buyers
a. Buyers in the ordinary course of business
b. Other buyers

E. Default

1. Sale of Collateral
2. Retention of Collateral

II. Suretyship

A. Nature and Formation

1. Types of Sureties
2. Formation

B. Rights of Surety

1. Exoneration
2. Reimbursement
3. Subrogation
4. Contribution

C. Defense of Surety

1. Personal Defenses of Principal Debtor
2. Personal Defenses of Surety
3. Defenses of Both Surety and Principal Debtor

Definitions

1. Secured transaction
2. Collateral
4. Security agreement
5. Security interest
6. Attachment
7. Perfection
8. Financing statement
9. Automatic perfection
10. Consumer goods
11. Equipment
12. Farm products
13. Inventory
14. Fixtures
15. Chattle paper
16. Instrument
17. Document
18. Account
19. General intangibles
20. Purchase money security interest
21. Surety
22. Absolute surety
23. Conditional guarantor
24. Exoneration
25. Reimbursement
26. Subrogation

True - False

_____ 1. A "secured party" may be either the seller of the goods or a third party creditor lender.

_____ 2. A security interest in property may continue even after the underlying debt is discharged.

_____ 3. A security interest can be perfected without attachment.

_____ 4. A security interest will be perfected if the interest has attached and the secured party files a financing statement signed by the creditor.

_____ 5. A purchase money security interest in consumer goods is perfected automatically upon attachment.

_____ 6. The Code's classifications of collateral as equipment and farm products are not mutually exclusive.

_____ 7. Unless the parties agree otherwise, a security agreement covering the debtor's inventory does not give the secured party rights to the proceeds from the sale of that inventory.

_____ 8. The Code determines whether and when goods become fixtures.

_____ 9. A security interest in goods represented by a negotiable document is perfected by negotiation of the document.

_____ 10. If two parties have unperfected security interests in the same collateral, the first to attach has priority.

_____ 11. A buyer in the ordinary course of business takes free of any security interest created by any previous seller of the collateral.

_____ 12. Unless the parties have otherwise agreed, after default the secured party may take possession of the collateral without judicial process if it can be done without a breach of the peace.

_____ 13. Unless the debtor waived his rights in the collateral before default, he has a right of redemption at any time before the secured party disposes of the collateral or enters into a contract to dispose of it.

_____ 14. Fidelity bonds guarantee the performance of the terms and conditions of a contract.

_____ 15. The principal debtor's mental incompentency is a valid defense of the principal debtor but not the surety.

Multiple Choice

_____ 1. Article 9 of the U.C.C. governs financing transactions involving security in all of the following except

a. tangible consumer goods
b. stocks and securities
c. real property
d. accounts receivable

_____ 2. A security interest "attaches" to the collateral in the security agreement only after

a. value is given to the debtor by the secured party
b. the debtor acquires rights in the collateral
c. the collateral is in the possession of the secured party or it is described in a security agreement signed by the debtor
d. all of the above

_____ 3. In general, a security interset in an instrument can be perfected by

a. the secured party's taking or retaining possession of the instrument
b. the secured's party filing a financing statement
c. either (a) or (b)
d. both (a) and (b)

_____ 4. Which of the following is not required for a financing statement to be effective?

a. the amount of the obligation secured
b. the names and addresses of the secured party and the debtor
c. a description of the collateral
d. the signature of the debtor

_____ 5. A tractor used by a farmer to plow his land, if collateral in which a security interest is granted is classified as

a. farm products
b. equipment
c. either (a) or (b)
d. both (a) and (b)

_____ 6. The term "inventory" includes

a. a retailer's merchandise
b. a manufacturer's raw materials
c. goods held for lease
d. all of the above

_____ 7. A creditor with an unperfected, but attached security interest has greater rights in the collateral than

a. the debtor's trustee in bankruptcy
b. the debtor's secured creditors
c. the debtor
d. none of the above

_____ 8. As between two parties with continuously perfected security interests in the same collateral, the party with the superior interest is that which

a. first filed a financing statement covering the collateral
b. first perfected his security interest
c. first did (a) or (b), whichever first occurred
d. first did (a) and (b), whichever first occurred

_____ 9. A perfected security interest has priority over claims of

a. lien creditors of the debtor
b. unsecured creditors of the debtor
c. the debtor himself
d. all of the above

_____10. On the debtor's default, the secured party may do all of the following except

a. foreclose on his claim
b. take possession of the collateral even if it requires a breach of the peace
c. reduce his claim to judgment
d. render the collateral useless on the debtor's premises

_____11. Upon the surety's payment of the principal debtor's entire obligation the surety obtains all the rights the creditor has against or through the principal debtor. This is the right of

a. exoneration
b. reimbursement
c. subrogation
d. contribution

_____12. Which of the following is not a personal defense of the surety

a. the surety's incapacity
b. the statute of frauds
c. the principal debtor's bankruptcy
d. fraud practiced by the creditor upon the surety

Short Essay

1. Outline briefly the steps that a lender must go through to attain a perfected security interest in a boat as collateral for a loan.

2. Would your answer in (1) differ if the collateral was (a) a house, (b) a sewing machine, (c) a car, (d) 100 shares of IBM stock? How?

3. What is a purchase money security interest in consumer goods? How is it perfected? When is the perfection effective?

36

BANKRUPTCY

Chapter Outline

I. Federal Bankruptcy Law

   A. Case Administration

      1. Commencement of the Case
         a. Voluntary petitions
         b. Involuntary petitions
      2. Automatic Stays
      3. Trustees
      4. Meetings of Creditors

   B. Creditors, The Debtor, and the Estate

      1. Creditors
         a. Proof of claims
         b. Secured claims
         c. Priority of claims
      2. Debtors
         a. Debtor's duties
         b. Debtor's exemptions
         c. Discharge
      3. The Estate
         a. Trustee as lien creditor
         b. Voidable preferences
         c. Fraudulent transfers
         d. Statutory liens

C. Liquidation

1. Proceedings
2. Distribution of the Estate
3. Discharge

D. Reorganization

1. Proceedings
2. Plan of Reorganization
3. Acceptance of Plan
4. Confirmation of Plan
   a. Good faith
   b. Feasibility
   c. Cash payments
   d. Acceptance by creditors
5. Effect of Reorganization

E. Adjustment of Debts of Individuals

1. Proceedings
2. The Plan
3. Confirmation
4. Discharge

II. Creditors' Rights and Debtor Relief Outside of Bankruptcy

A. Compositions

B. Assignments for Benefit of Creditors

C. Statutory Assignments

D. Equity Receiverships

Definitions

1. Voluntary petition
2. Involuntary petition
3. Trustee
4. Claim
5. Secured claim
6. Unsecured claim
7. Discharge
8. Voidable preference
9. Insider
10. Transfer
11. Liquidation
12. Reorganization
13. Confirmation of plan
14. Adjustment of debts of individuals
15. Composition
16. Assignment for benefit of creditors
17. Receivership
18. Subordination of claims
19. Judicial lien
20. Insolvency
21. Statutory lien

True - False

_____ 1. Federal bankruptcy law is generally superseded by State insolvency laws

_____ 2. Chapter 13 of the Bankruptcy Act applies to individuals with regular income who owe liquidated unsecured debts of less than $100,000 and secured debts of less than $350,000.

_____ 3. The jurisdiction of the bankruptcy court and the operation of the bankruptcy laws are commenced by the filing of a voluntary or involuntary petition.

_____ 4. A debtor must be insolvent before he can file a voluntary petition.

_____ 5. As the representative of the estate, the trustee in bankruptcy has the capacity to sue or to be sued.

_____ 6. A secured creditor's claim is secured to the extent of the allowed amount of his claim, even if that amount exceeds the value of his interest in the debtor's property.

_____ 7. After creditors with secured claims and creditors with claims having a priority have been satisfied, creditors with allowed, unsecured claims share proportionately in any remaining assets.

_____ 8. The debtor's estate in bankruptcy includes any property received by the debtor by inheritance or as a beneficiary of a life insurance policy within one year after commencement of the case.

_____ 9. All transfers made by the debtor within ninety days of bankruptcy are voidable.

_____ 10. Any person that may be a debtor under Chapter 7 and railroads may be a debtor under Chapter 11.

_____ 11. Under Chapter 11, the debtor will remain in possession of and management of the property of the estate unless the court appoints a trustee, who then may operate the debtor's business.

_____ 12. A plan of reorganization under Chapter 11 need not be confirmed by the court to be binding on the parties.

_____ 13. A composition is an alternative method of settling a debtor's estate under the Bankruptcy Act.

_____ 14. A plan under Chapter 13 will not be confirmed by the bankruptcy court if the value of the property to be distributed to unsecured creditors under the plan is less than they would receive under Chapter 7.

Multiple Choice

_____ 1. The Chapter of the Bankruptcy Act containing the provisions dealing with case administration is

a. Chapter 1
b. Chapter 3
c. Chapter 4
d. Chapter 5

_____ 2. Chapter 7 of the Bankruptcy Act is entitled

a. liquidation
b. adjustment of debts of a municipality
c. reorganization
d. adjustments of debts of an individual with regular income

_____ 3. Chapter 7 of the Bankruptcy Act applies to all debtors except

a. railroads
b. insurance companies
c. homestead associations
d. all of the above

_____ 4. Which of the following is not a duty or power of a trustee under the Bankruptcy Act?

a. to use, sell or lease property of the estate
b. to deposit or invest money of the estate
c. to conduct the affairs of the debtor's estate for the trustee's own benefit
d. to assume or reject any executory contract or unexpired lease of the debtor

_____ 5. The Bankruptcy Court will not allow a creditor's claim when the claim

a. is unenforceable against the debtor and his property
b. is for an interest that has not yet matured
c. may be offset against a debt owing the debtor
d. all of the above

_____ 6. A creditor's claim will be denied by the Bankruptcy Court as that of an insider if the creditor is any of the following except

a. a general partner of the debtor
b. a partnership in which the debtor is a limited partner
c. a relative of the debtor
d. a corporation of which the debtor is a director

_____ 7. Which of the following items of the debtor's property is <u>not</u> exempted from the bankruptcy proceedings by the Bankruptcy Act?

a. social security benefits
b. future wages
c. unemployment compensation
d. all of the above

_____ 8. The following debts are <u>not</u> dischargeable in a bankruptcy proceeding <u>except</u>

a. alimony and support of a spouse or child
b. student loans that first became due less than five years before the filing of the bankruptcy petition
c. accounts payable due less than six months before the filing of the bankruptcy petition
d. none of the debts

_____ 9. The estate in bankruptcy includes property that the trustee recovers under his powers

a. as a lien creditor
b. to avoid a voidable preference
c. to avoid a fraudulent transfer
d. all of the above

_____10. The trustee may avoid a fraudulent transfer made by the debtor on or within ______ before the date of the filing of the petition.

a. sixty days
b. ninety days
c. one hundred and eighty days
d. one year

_____11. Under Chapter 7 of the Bankruptcy Act, after secured creditors collect on their security interests, the next to receive assets from the estate in bankruptcy is/are

a. the debtor
b. unsecured creditors who file their claims on time
c. the trustee, for his services
d. creditors entitled to a priority

_____12. A court will confirm a plan of reorganization under Chapter 11 of the Bankruptcy Act only if it meets all of the requirements of the Act, including all of the following <u>except</u>

a. The plan must be accepted by all of the creditors.
b. Certain classes of creditors must have their allowed claims paid in full in cash immediately, or in some instances, upon a deferred basis.
c. The court must find that the plan is feasible.
d. The plan must have been proposed in good faith.

Short Essay

1. Identify and describe briefly each of the steps involved in the administration of a case under Chapter 3 of the Bankruptcy Act.

2. What is the effect of a discharge of a debt? When is an agreement to enforce a discharged debt enforceable?

3. Describe briefly the role of a trustee in bankruptcy as a lien creditor.

4. Under what conditions can a trustee recover a preferential transfer made to a creditor?

5. Identify and discuss briefly three non-bankruptcy forms of compromises that have been developed to provide relief to debtors.

37

TRADE REGULATION

Chapter Outline

I. Antitrust

   A. Sherman Antitrust Act

      1. Contracts, Combinations, and Conspiracies in Restraint of Trade

         a. Price fixing
         b. Market allocations
         c. Boycotts
         d. Tying arrangements

      2. Monopolies

         a. Monopolization
         b. Attempts to monopolize

   B. Clayton Act

      1. Tying Arrangements and Exclusive Dealing
      2. Mergers
      3. Interlocking Directorates

   C. Robinson - Patman Act

      1. Cost Justification
      2. Meeting Competition

   D. Federal Trade Commission Act

II. Unfair Competition

A. Trade Secrets

B. Trade-marks, Marks, and Trade Names

1. Trade-marks
2. Service Marks, Certification Marks, Collective Marks
3. Trade Names

C. Copyrights and Patents

1. Copyrights
2. Patents

Definitions

1. Rule of reason test
2. Per se test
3. Horizontal restraint
4. Vertical restraint
5. Retail price maintenance
6. Tying arrangement
7. Monopoly
8. Attempt to monopolize
9. Interlocking directorate
10. Price discrimination
11. Trade-mark
12. Trade name
13. Copyright
14. Patent

True - False

_____ 1. State courts are empowered to issue injunctions restraining violations of the Sherman Act.

_____ 2. Under the Sherman Act, those restraints not characterized as *per se* illegal are judged by the Rule of Reason test.

_____ 3. The Sherman Act prohibits sellers' agreements not to advertise their prices.

_____ 4. While the Sherman Act prohibits sellers' agreements to establish minimum prices, sellers are free to agree to establish maximum prices.

_____ 5. Under the Sherman Act, the refusal of a seller to deal with any particular buyer is considered illegal *per se*.

_____ 6. Because of their tendency to exclude competitors from the market, all tying arrangements have been declared illegal *per se*.

_____ 7. Under the Robinson-Patman Act, liability may be imposed upon buyers as well as sellers.

_____ 8. Restrictive employment agreements are enforced by the courts if their time and area limitations are reasonable.

_____ 9. Under the Trade-mark Act of 1946, a trade mark is required to be affixed to the goods it identifies.

_____10. The granting of a patent guarantees the patentee the exclusive right to make, use, or sell his invention.

Multiple Choice

_____ 1. Violators of the Sherman Act are subject to

a. fines and imprisonment
b. injunctions
c. civil actions for treble damages
d. all of the above

_____ 2. The Rule of Reason test is used to determine the legality of

a. horizontal price fixing agreements
b. vertical territorial and custsomer restrictions
c. horizontal market allocation agreements
d. retail price maintenance agreements

_____ 3. A company is not in possession of monopoly power if its share of the market is

a. 100%
b. 85%
c. 75%
d. 50%

_____ 4. Labor unions are exempted from the antitrust laws by

a. the Sherman Act
b. the Clayton Act
c. the Robinson-Patman Act
d. the FTC Act

_____ 5. A company which unilaterally fixes prices has violated

a. the Sherman Act
b. the Clayton Act
c. the FTC Act
d. none of the above

_____ 6. A person who knowingly induces or receives an illegal discrimination in price has violated

a. the Sherman Act
b. the Clayton Act
c. the Robinson-Patman Act
d. none of the above

_____ 7. A corporation which acquires the stock of another corporation where the effect may be substantially to lessen competition between the two corporations has violated

a. the Sherman Act
b. the Clayton Act
c. the Robinson-Patman Act
d. the FTC Act

_____ 8. A company which engages in unfair methods of competition has violated

a. the Sherman Act
b. the Clayton Act
c. the Robinson-Patman Act
d. the FTC Act

_____ 9. Membership in a trade union is generally indicated by

a. a trade-mark
b. a service mark
c. a collective mark
d. a certification mark

_____ 10. A patent is valid for a period of

a. 17 years
b. the inventor's life plus 17 years
c. 50 years
d. the inventor's life plus 50 years

Short Essay

1. What is the purpose of the Federal and State antitrust statutes?

2. According to economic theory, how does a monopolistic market differ from a competitive market?

3. What must be shown to prove a company guilty of monopolization under Section 2 of the Sherman Act?

4. What must be shown to prove a company guilty of an attempt to monopolize under Section 2 of the Sherman Act?

38

SECURITIES REGULATION

Chapter Outline

A. The Securities Act of 1933

1. Definition of a Security
2. Registration of Securities
3. Exempt Securities
   a. Regulation A
   b. Intra-state issues
   c. Short-term commercial paper
   d. Other exempt securities
4. Exempt Transactions
   a. Private placements
   b. Limited offers not exceeding $5,000,000
   c. Limited offers not exceeding $500,000
   d. Limited Offers Solely to Accredited Investors
   e. Resales of restricted securities
5. Liability
   a. Unregistered sales
   b. False registration statements
   c. Anti-fraud provision
   d. Criminal sanctions

B. The Securities Exchange Act of 1934

1. Registration and Periodic Reporting Requirements
2. Anti-fraud Provision
   a. Requisites of Rule 10b-5
   b. Insider Trading
3. Short Swing Profits
4. Proxy Solicitations
5. Tender Offers

6. Foreign Corrupt Practices Act
    a. Accounting requirements
    b. Anti-bribery provisions

C. Accountant's Legal Liability

1. Common Law
    a. Contract liability
    b. Tort Liability
    c. Criminal Liability
    d. Client Information
2. Federal Securities Law
    a. 1933 Act
    b. 1934 Act

Definitions

1. Blue sky laws
2. Prospectus
3. Security
4. Offering circular
5. Intra-state issue
6. Nonexclusive safe harbor
7. Restricted securities
8. Reasonable care
9. Private placement
10. Accredited purchases
11. Due diligence
12. Short swing profits
13. Insider
14. Scienter
15. Inside information
16. Tippee
17. Proxy
18. Proxy statement
19. Tender offer
20. Shelf Registration

True - False

_____ 1. A registrant may lawfully sell its securities immediately upon filing its registration statement with the SEC.

_____ 2. Exempt securities may be resold without registration.

_____ 3. The exemption for intra-state issues is not available if one or more offerees are not a resident of the state in which the issuer is resident.

_____ 4. Securities sold in an exempt transaction may be resold only by registration.

_____ 5. Securities sold under the private placement exemption may be purchased by an unlimited number of purchasers.

_____ 6. An issuer need not notify the SEC of sales made pursuant to an exempt transaction.

_____ 7. A person who purchases a security sold in violation of the registration requirement of the 1933 Act has the right to tender it back to the seller and recover the purchase price.

_____ 8. The Securities Exchange Act of 1934 applies only to companies whose assets exceed $3 million and who have a class of equity securities with 500 or more shareholders.

_____ 9. Under the 1934 Act, all regulated publicly held companies must make a one-time registration with the SEC.

_____ 10. Under Rule 10b-5, liability may be imposed upon buyers as well as sellers.

_____ 11. Fines imposed upon individuals for violations of the Foreign Corrupt Practices Act may not be paid by the issuing corporation.

_____ 12. The only contract duties an accountant incurs are those he explicitly agrees to render.

_____ 13. Privity of contract is a requirement to a cause of action against an accountant based upon fraud.

_____ 14. An accountant is permitted to disclose confidential communications from his client if a court orders the disclosure.

Multiple Choice

_____ 1. The effective date of a registration statement is

a. the day it is filed with the SEC
b. the tenth day after it is filed with the SEC
c. the twentieth day after it is filed with the SEC
d. none of the above

_____ 2. Under Regulation A, an issuer may make a yearly offering of unregistered securities of up to

a. $5000,000
b. $1,500,000
c. $5,000,000
d. none of the above

_____ 3. The exemption for short-term commercial paper is not available if

a. the security has a maturity at the time of issuance of less than nine months
b. the proceeds are to be used for working capital
c. the proceeds are to be used for the acquisition of capital equipment
d. (a) and (c) but not (b)

_____ 4. Which of the following securities must be registered?

a. securities of domestic governments
b. securities of domestic banks
c. securities of not-for-profit, charitable organizations
d. none of the above

_____ 5. Under Rule 506 of the SEC, an issuer may make a private placement of unregistered securities of up to

a. $500,000
b. $1,500,000
c. $5,000,000
d. none of the above

_____ 6. Violators of the 1933 Act are subject to

a. administrative remedies by the SEC
b. civil liability to injured investors
c. criminal penalties
d. all of the above

_____ 7. There are <u>no</u> defenses to

a. selling an unregistered security which is required to be registered
b. including in a registration statement any untrue statement or omission of material fact
c. selling a security by means of a prospectus which includes an untrue statement of material fact or an omission of a material fact
d. (b) and (c) but not (a)

_____ 8. Corporate insiders who buy the stock of the corporation will be liable to the corporation for any profits made pursuant to a sale of that stock within

a. 20 days
b. 90 days
c. 6 months
d. 12 months

_____ 9. Assume Y, an officer of the C corporation, buys 700 shares of C stock on January 1 for $10 per share and 800 shares of C stock on March 15 for $8 per share. If Y then sells 600 of these shares on June 30 for $12 per share and the remaining 900 shares on October 15 for $14 per share, Y will be liable to C for

a. $1,200
b. $2,000
c. $2,400
d. $4,000

_____ 10. A person will <u>not</u> be liable for a violation of Rule 10b-5 if his misconduct was

a. intentional
b. reckless
c. negligent
d. none of the above

_____ 11. Management may omit a shareholder proposal from its proxy statement if the proposal

a. is a proper subject for shareholder action
b. is significantly related to the business of the issuer
c. relates to the conduct of the ordinary business operations of the issuer
d. all of the above

Short Essay

1. What is the primary purpose of Federal securities regulation?

2. What information must typically be disclosed in a registration statement?

3. What steps must an issuer take to assure against non-exempt, unregistered resales of restricted securities?

4. How is the profit from a short-swing sale calculated?

39

CONSUMER PROTECTION

<u>Chapter Outline</u>

A. Unfair and Deceptive Trade Practices

B. Consumer Purchases

   1. Federal Warranty Protection
   2. Consumer Right of Rescission

C. Consumer Credit Obligations

   1. Access to the Market
   2. Disclosure Requirements
   3. Contract Terms
   4. Fair Reportage
   5. Creditors' Remedies

D. Consumer Health and Safety

Definitions

1. Consumer transaction
2. Caveat emptor
3. Full warranty
4. Limited warranty
5. Property report
6. Open-ended credit account
7. Closed-ended credit account
8. Billing error
9. Finance charge
10. Authorized additional charge
11. Pre-payment
12. Balloon payment
13. Holder in due course
14. Delinquency charge
15. Wage assignment
16. Garnishment
17. Deficiency judgment

True - False

_____ 1. Orders of the Federal Trade Commission are <u>not</u> subject to jucidial review

_____ 2. Under the FTC Act, a person may be guilty of deceptive advertising even though no one is proved to have been actually deceived.

_____ 3. Under the Magnuson-Moss Warranty Act, a written warranty can <u>not</u> disclaim or modify any implied warranty.

_____ 4. A contract subject to the Interstate Land Sales Full Disclosure Act must clearly provide that the contract may be revoked at the option of the purchaser within two years of signing the contract.

_____ 5. Violators of the Equal Credit Opportunity Act are subject to civil actions to recover actual and punitive damages.

_____ 6. Federal disclosure standards relating to credit terms for consumer loans must be complied with in every State.

_____ 7. The Fair Credit Billing Act requires creditors to explain or correct billing errors.

_____ 8. Most States impose statutory ceilings on the amount that may be charged for the extension of consumer credit.

_____ 9. Under the Fair Credit Reporting Act, a consumer is entitled to read and copy all information pertaining to him in the consumer reporting agency's files.

_____10. The Consumer Credit Protection Act prohibits wage assignments.

_____11. The Fair Debt Collection Practices Act prohibits debt collection conduct by debt collectors other than the creditor that is harrassing, oppressive, or abusive.

Multiple Choice

_____ 1. Under the FTC Act, complaints are normally instituted by

a. the Federal Trade Commission
b. the injured party
c. the Attorney General of the State in which the injured party is resident
d. none of the above

_____ 2. Under the Magnuson-Moss Warranty Act, a written warranty that limits the duration of implied warranties may be designated

a. "full" but not "limited"
b. "limited" but not "full"
c. "full" or "limited"
d. none of the above

_____ 3. Under the Magnuson-Moss Warranty Act, a seller may disclaim any and all implied warranties if

a. he gives no written warranty
b. the product is for personal use only
c. the product costs $10 or less
d. none of the above

_____ 4. Under the FTC's door-to-door sales rule, a consumer may only revoke a door-to-door sales contract if

a. the sale is on credit
b. any credit obligation he incurs pursuant to the contract is secured by a mortgage on his home
c. the sale is for $25 or more
d. all of the above

_____ 5. Which of the following acts requires a creditor, within thirty days of receiving an application for credit, to notify the applicant of action taken and to provide specific reasons for a denial of credit?

a. Consumer Credit Protection Act
b. Equal Credit Opportunity Act
c. Fair Credit Reporting Act
d. Fair Credit Billing Act

_____ 6. The Equal Credit Opportunity Act prohibits businesses that regularly extend credit from discriminating in extending credit on the basis of

a. sex
b. marital status
c. age
d. all of the above

_____ 7. Under the Consumer Credit Protection Act, sales finance charges and interest rates must be quoted in terms of

a. add-ons
b. discounts
c. annual percentage rates
d. none of the above

_____ 8. Which of the following acts prohibits kickbacks and referral fees with respect to federally related mortgage loans?

a. Interstate Land Sales Full Disclosure Act
b. Real Estate Settlement Procedures Act
c. Fair Credit Billing Act
d. Consumer Credit Protection Act

_____ 9. A creditor who fails to respond to a billing error complaint may <u>not</u>

a. take any action to collect the disputed amount
b. restrict the use of a revolving credit account because the disputed amount is unpaid
c. report the disputed amount as delinquent
d. all of the above

_____10. The Consumer Credit Protection Act limits a credit card holder's liability for unauthorized use of a credit card to

a. $10
b. $25
c. $50
d. none of the above

Short Essay

1. What must a warrantor do to comply with the Magnuson-Moss Warranty Act?

2. What are the characteristics of a "full" warranty under the Magnuson-Moss Warranty Act?

3. What information must a creditor give to a consumer who is opening an open-ended credit account?

4. What information must a creditor give to a consumer who is opening a closed-ended credit account?

5. Under what circumstances may a credit card issuer collect from a credit card holder for unauthorized use of a credit card?

40

INTRODUCTION TO REAL AND PERSONAL PROPERTY

Chapter Outline

I. Introduction to Property

   A. Kinds of Property

      1. Tangible and Intangible Property
      2. Real and Personal Property
      3. Fixtures

   B. Incidents of Property Ownership

      1. Transfer of Property During Life
      2. Devolution of Title on Death of Owner
      3. Taxation

II. Personal Property

   A. Transfer of Title

      1. By Sale
      2. By Gift
         a. Delivery
         b. Intent
         c. Acceptance
      3. By Will or Descent
      4. By Accession
      5. By Confusion
      6. By Possession

   B. Concurrent Ownership

Definitions

1. Property

2. Tangible property

3. Intangible property

4. Real property

5. Personal property

6. Fixture

7. Gift

8. Donor

9. Donee

10. Constructive Delivery

11. Accession

12. Confusion of goods

13. Lost properety

15. Concurrent ownership

True - False

_____ 1. All property interests that are not classified as real property or as fixtures are classified as personal property.

_____ 2. The intention of the parties with conflicting claims to the property, as expressed in their agreement, is controlling in determining whether personal property has become a fixture.

_____ 3. A tenant may remove trade fixtures provided he can do so without causing material injury to the real property to which it is affixed.

_____ 4. In general, a gratuitous promise to make a gift is binding.

_____ 5. To be effective, a gift must be physically transferred or "delivered" to the donee.

_____ 6. Although acceptance by the donee is a requirement of a valid gift, the law generally presumes that the donee has accepted the gift.

_____ 7. If X deliberately takes Y's lumber and builds a boat, Y recieves title to the boat by accession.

_____ 8. If confusion of goods results by accident and there is not enough left to distribute a full share to each owner, each party will lose his entire interest if he cannot prove his share.

_____ 9. In general, a finder has superior title to lost property as against everyone but the true owner.

_____ 10. Only real property may be held concurrently by two or more persons.

Multiple Choice

_____ 1. An automobile is classified as

a. tangible property
b. personal property
c. both (a) and (b)
d. neither (a) or (b)

_____ 2. All of the following may be classified as tangible, personal property except

a. a watch
b. a bank check
c. a dog
d. a pencil

_____ 3. In the absence of a binding agreement between the parties, the court, in determining whether an item is a fixture, will consider the following factors

a. the physical relationship of the item to the land
b. the intention of the person who attached the item to the land
c. the interest of the person who attached the item to the land at the time of attachment
d. all of the above

_____ 4. In determining whether an item is a fixture, the test of "purpose or use" applies only if the item

a. is affixed to the realty in some way
b. can be removed without material injury to the realty
c. either (a) or (b)
d. both (a) and (b)

_____ 5. The distinction between real and personal property is important in that legal consequences follow from it in the area(s) of

a. transfer of property during one's life
b. transfer of property on one's death
c. taxation of property interests
d. all of the above

_____ 6. The basic distinction between a gift and a sale is that a gift

a. requires delivery
b. lacks any consideration
c. requires intent on the part of the donor
d. must be accepted by the donee

_____ 7. Which of the requirements of an effective gift is presumed?

a. delivery to be donee
b. intent on donor's part to make a present gift
c. acceptance by the donee
d. none of the above

_____ 8. Under the dcotrine of title by accession, if X innocently took Y's lumber and constructed a boat, and the value of Y's labor is greater than the value of X's raw lumber

a. X is entitled to recover the boat and does not have to compensate Y for the reasonable value of the improvements
b. X is entitled to recover the boat but he must compensate Y for the reasonable value of the improvements
c. X is not entitled to recover the boat but he can seek money damages for the value of the lumber
d. X is not entitled to recover the boat and he cannot seek money damages for the value of the lumber

_____ 9. Under the doctrine of confusion, if X, Y, and Z accidently commingle identical cases of beer, and there is not enought left to distribute a full share to each

a. the first owners proving their proportion of the whole are entitled to receive their share
b. the loss will be born by each in proportion to his share
c. no party will recover anything unless he can prove his share
d. none of the above

_____10. X promises to give a ring to Y, but loses it before he gives it to her. Z then finds the ring, and both X and Y claim it. Who is entitled to the right?

a. X
b. Y
c. Z
d. X and Y jointly

Short Essay

1. Distinguish between real property, personal property, and fixtures; between tangible and intangible property. What is the legal significance, if any, of these distinctions ?

2. How does a court determine whether an item is personal property or a fixture?

3. Distinguish between a gift and a sale.

41

BAILMENTS AND DOCUMENTS OF TITLE

Chapter Outline

I. Bailments

   A. Essential Elements of a Bailment

      1. Delivery of Possession
      2. Personal Property
      3. Possession for a Determinable Time
         a. Sales
         b. Conditional sales
         c. Other transfers of title
      4. Restoration of Possession to the Bailor

   B. Rights and Duties of Bailor and Bailee

      1. Bailee's Duty to Exercise Due Care
      2. Bailee's Absolute Liability
      3. Bailee's Rights to Compensation

   C. Speical Kinds of Bailments

      1. Pledges
      2. Warehousing
      3. Carriers of Goods
         a. Duty to carry
         b. Liability for loss or damage
         c. Duty to deliver to the right person
      4. Innkeepers

II. Documents of Title

A. Types of Documents of Title

1. Warehouse Receipts
   a. Duties of Warehousemen
   b. Lien of Warehouseman
2. Bills of Lading
   a. Duties of issuer of bill of lading
   b. Through bills of lading
   c. Lien of carrier

B. Negotiability of Documents of Title

1. Due Negotiation
2. Rights Acquired by Due Negotiation
3. Rights Acquired in the Absence of Due Negotiation
4. Warranties
5. Ineffective Documents of Title
6. Lost or Missing Documents of Title

Definitions

1. Bailment
2. Bailor
3. Bailee
4. Bailment for sole benefit of bailor
5. Bailment for sole benefit of bailee
6. Bailment for mutual benefit
7. Pledge
8. Warehouseman
9. Contract carrier
10. Common carrier
11. Innkeeper
12. Document of title
13. Bill of lading
14. Warehouse receipt
15. Through bill of lading
16. Negotiability
17. Due negotiation

True - False

_____ 1. A bailment relationship can exist with respect to both real and personal property.

_____ 2. In order to establish a bailment relationship, the person receiving possession of the property must be under a duty to return the property.

_____ 3. The bailee has the exclusive right to possess the bailed goods for the term of the bailment.

_____ 4. Almost every State has by statute adopted the common law rule that a bailee loses his lien on the bailed goods upon their redelivery to the bailor.

_____ 5. A private carrier has no duty to accept goods for carriage except where it has agreed to do so by contract.

_____ 6. The extent of a warehouseman's liability for misdelivery may be limited by a provision in the warehouse receipt fixing a specific maximum liability.

_____ 7. A warehouseman has a lien on the goods to enforce the payment of his charges and any necessary expenses incurred in keeping and handling the goods.

_____ 8. The liability of the originating carrier that receives the goods from the shipper for loss or damage is limited to the period while the goods are in its possession.

_____ 9. After an indorsement in blank or to bearer, a negotiable document of title may be negotiated by delivery alone.

_____10. A carrier or warehouseman, who receives goods from a finder and later delivers them to the person to whom the thief ordered, is liable to the true owner of the goods.

_____11. If, in the absence of a court order a carrier delivers goods to a person claiming them under a missing negotiable document, it is liable to anyone who is injured by its actions.

Multiple Choice

_____ 1. X gives his car to Y so that Y can take it to the garage to be repaired by Z. This is an example of

a. a mutual benefit bailment
b. a bailment for the sole benefit of the bailee
c. a bailment for the sole benefit of the bailor
d. all of the above

_____ 2. Which of the following is not an essential element of a bailment relationship?

a. delivery of lawful opssession of specific personal property by the bailor to the bailee
b. transfer of title to the property from the bailor to the bailee for a determinable period of time
c. an obligation of the bailee to return the property to the bailee or to one with a superior right of possession at the end of the bailment
d. all of the above are essential elements of a bailment relationship

_____ 3. A mutual benefit bailment will terminate on the happening of any of the conditions listed below except

a. when the purpose of the bailment is fully accomplished
b. when the time for which the bailment was created expires
c. when the bailed goods are destroyed
d. all of the above

_____ 4. A bailee is free from liability for casualty to the bailed goods if he exercised the requisite degree of care unless he

a. agrees with the bailor to insure the goods against a certain risk, then failed to do so and the casualty to the goods occurred through such a risk
b. used the bailed property in a manner not authorized by the bailment and damage results from that use
c. delivers the property to the wrong person by mistake
d. all of the above

_____ 5. In order for a carrier to be subject to the rules applicable to common carriers, all of the following conditions must be present except that

a. the carriage must be a part of its business
b. the majority of the carrier's business must be as a common carrier
c. the carriage must be for renumeration
d. the carrier must represent to the general public that it is willing to serve the public in the transportation of property

_____ 6. A bill of lading serves as

a. a receipt for the goods transported
b. evidence of the contract of carriage
c. a document of title
d. all of the above

_____ 7. A document of title is negotiable if it is made payable to any of the following <u>except</u>

a. to a named person
b. to bearer
c. to order
d. a document of title is negotiable if made payable to any of the above

_____ 8. A holder of a negotiable document of title to whom it has been duly negotiated obtains all of the following <u>except</u>

a. title to the document
b. proof that the document is genuine
c. title to the goods
d. the holder has all of the above rights

_____ 9. A person who transfers a document of title for value to other than a collecting bank or other intermediary warrants to his immediate purchaser that

a. the document is genuine
b. he has no knowledge of any fact that would impair the validity or worth of the document
c. his transfer is rightful and fully effective with respect to the document of title and the goods it represents
d. all of the above

_____ 10. A purchaser will obtain title to goods by negotiation to him of a document of title provided the goods have been delivered to the issuer of the document by

a. a finder of the goods
b. a thief of the goods
c. the true owner of the goods
d. none of the above

Short Essay

1. Identify the four requirements for a bailment relationship to exist.

2. What are the three baisc kinds of bailments and what standard is applied to the bailee's duty to exercise due care under each?

3. What does a bailor have to show to recover from the bailee for goods that are returned damaged?

4. Compare and contrast the duties and liabilities of a common carrier with those of a private carrier.

42

INTERESTS IN REAL PROPERTY

Chapter Outline

I. Freehold Estates

  A. Fee Estates

    1. Fee Simple Estate
    2. Base or Qualified Fee Estate

  B. Life Estates

    1. Conventional Life Estates
    2. Life Estates Established by Law
      a. Dower
      b. Curtesy

  C. Future Interests

    1. Reversions
    2. Remainders
      a. Vested remainders
      b. Contingent remainders

II. Leasehold Estates

  A. Creation and Duration of the Leasehold Estate

    1. Definite Term
    2. Periodic Tenancy
    3. Tenancy at Will
    4. Tenancy at Sufferance

B. Transfer of Interests in a Leasehold

1. Transfers by Landlord
2. Transfers by Tenant
   a. Assignment
   b. Sublease

C. Tenant's Obligations

1. Effect of Destruction of the Premises
2. Effect of Eviction or Abandonment
   a. Dispossession by landlord for breach of contract
   b. Wrongful abandonment by tenant
   c. Wrongful eviction by landlord

D. Landlord's Obligations

1. Quiet Enjoyment
2. Fitness for Use
3. Repair

III. Concurrent Ownership

A. Joint Tenancy

B. Tenancy in Common

C. Tenancy by the Entireties

D. Community Property

E. Condominiums

F. Cooperatives

IV. Nonpossessory Interests

A. Easements

1. Types of Easements
2. Creation of Easements
   a. Express grant or reservation
   b. Implied grant or reservation
   c. Necessity
   d. Dedication
   e. Prescription

B. Profits A Prendre

C. Licenses

Definitions

1. Freehold estate

2. Leasehold estate

3. Fee simple estate

4. Qualified fee estate

5. Conventional life estate

6. Future interest

7. Reversion

8. Remainder

9. Estate for years

10. Periodic tenancy

11. Tenancy at will

12. Tenancy at sufferance

13. Assignment of a lease

14. Sublease

15. Constructive eviction

16. Tenancy in common

17. Joint tenancy

18. Tenancy by the entireties

19. Community property

20. Condominiums

21. Cooperatives

22. Easements

23. Profit a prendre

24. License

True - False

_____ 1. Both freehold estates and leasehold estates are regarded as possessory interests in property.

_____ 2. A fee simple estate is created by any words which indicate an intent to convey absolute ownership.

_____ 3. A widow's common law dower is subordinate to claims that were not reduced to a judgment before marriage.

_____ 4. A reversion, a life estate, and a remainder are all considered future interests.

_____ 5. A lease is both a contract and a grant of an estate in land.

_____ 6. A lease that does not specify any duration is treated as a tenancy at sufferance.

_____ 7. Unless specifically permitted in the lease, leases are not freely assignable without the landlord's consent.

_____ 8. A tenant is under no duty to make any repairs to the leased premises unless the lease expressly so provides.

_____ 9. Like joint tenants, tenants in common are persons who hold undivided interests in the property, each having the right to possession, but neither claiming any specific portion of the property.

_____ 10. A tenancy by the entireties can only be created in a conveyance to a husband and wife.

_____ 11. The purchaser of a cooperative acquires separate ownership to the unit and becomes a tenant in common in the common facilities.

_____ 12. It is generally the responsibility of the owner of the servient parcel to maintain the easement and keep it in repair.

Multiple Choice

_____ 1. All of the following conveyances will create an unqualified fee simple estate in the transferee except

a. "To B"
b. "To B forever"
c. "To B so long as she does not remarry"
d. "To B in fee simple"

_____ 2. If B is given a life estate in Blackacre by A, and B then sells his entire interest in Blackacre to C, C's interest in Blackacre is

a. a fee simple estate
b. a qualified fee simple estate
c. a life estate for B's life
d. a life estate for C's life

_____ 3. O conveys Greenacre "to A for life, then to B". What interest, if any, does B have in Greenacre?

a. a reversion
b. a vested remainder
c. a contingent remainder
d. no interest

_____ 4. A leases a factory to B for 3 years. The written lease provides that rent is to be paid on the first day of each month, and that either party may terminate the lease at any time. The lease can best be described as

a. an estate for years
b. a periodic tenancy "from year to year"
c. a periodic tenancy "from month to month"
d. a tenancy at will

_____ 5. After he conveys the leasehold interest, the landlord may transfer to a third party his

a. reversionary interest in the leasehold
b. right to rent to be paid by the tenant
c. neither (a) nor (b)
d. both (a) and (b)

_____ 6. If a tenant assigns his leasehold interest without the written consent of the landlord as required by the lease, the assignment is

a. valid and enforceable
b. void and unenforceable by either party
c. voidable at the landlord's election
d. treated as a sublease

_____ 7. A tenancy in common requires which of the following "unities"?

a. time
b. title
c. interest
d. possession

_____ 8. A conveys "the back forty" to B. The parcel is bordered on three sides by the remainder of A's farm and on the fourth by a river. At present, B has no access to the highway and the deed from A grants none. Which of the following is correct?

a. B has an express easement across A's land to the highway
b. B has an implied easement across A's land to the highway
c. B has an easement by necessity across A's land to the highway
d. B has no right to cross A's land to the highway

_____ 9. If A gives B permission to extract oil from his land, he has given B

a. an easement in gross
b. a license
c. a profit a prendre
d. none of the above

_____10. A theatre ticket is an example of

a. an easement in gross
b. a license
c. a profit a prendre
d. none of the above

Short Essay

1. What are the basic characteristics of a fee simple estate? How do these estates differ from a qualified fee simple estate?

2. Distinguish among a reversion, a possibility of reverter, and a remainder.

3. How do the rights and duties of the parties to an assignment of a lease differ from those of the parties to a sublease?

4. What are the rights and duties of the landlord and tenant at common law? How have most jurisdictions changed these rules?

5. What are the two types of easements? How do they differ from each other? From a profit pendre? From a license?

43

TRANSFER AND CONTROL OF REAL PROPERTY

Chapter Outline

I. Transfer of Real Property

   A. Contract for Sale

      1. Formation
      2. Marketable Title

   B. Deeds

      1. Types of Deeds
         a. Warranty deed
         b. Special warranty deed
         c. Quitclaim deed
      2. Formal Requirements
         a. Consideration
         b. Description of the land
         c. Quantity of the estate
         d. Covenants of title
         e. Execution
      3. Delivery of Deeds
      4. Recordation

   C. Secured Transactions

      1. Form of Mortgages
      2. Rights and Duties
      3. Transfer of the Interests under the Mortgage
      4. Foreclosure

   D. Adverse Possession

II. Public and Private Controls

A. Zoning

1. Enabling Acts and Zoning Ordinances
2. Variance
3. Non-conforming Uses
4. Judicial Review of Zoning
5. Subdivision Master Plans

B. Eminent Domain

1. Public Use
2. Just Compensation

C. Private Restrictions Upon Land Use

1. Nature of Restrictive Covenants
2. Type and Construction of Restrictive Covenants
3. Termination of Restrictive Covenants
4. Validity of Restrictive Covenants

Definitions

1. Marketable title

2. Warranty deed

3. Special warranty deed

4. Quitclaim deed

5. Mortgagor

6. Mortgagee

7. Deed of trust

8. Right of redemption

9. Adverse possession

10. Variance

11. Non-conforming use

12. Eminent domain

13. Restrictive covenant

True - False

_____ 1. Title to land may only be transferred by deed.

_____ 2. To be enforceable, a contract for the sale of an interest in land must be in writing and signed by the party against whom enforcement is sought.

_____ 3. At common law, when the contract of sale is entered into, the risk of loss or destruction of the proprty passes to the purchaser.

_____ 4. In most jurisdictions, consideration must pass between the parties for a deed to be valid.

_____ 5. A deed is not effective to pass title unless and until it is both delivered and recorded.

_____ 6. The provisions of Article 9 of the U.C.C. govern real estate mortgages and trust deeds.

_____ 7. A mortgagee has the right to assign the mortgage to a third person without the consent of the mortgagor.

_____ 8. When the power of eminent domain is exercised, the award of compensation is given to the holders of all vested and contingent interests in the condemmed property.

_____ 9. In a notice-race State, an unrecorded is invalid against any subsequent purchaser without notice who records first.

_____10. Under a special warranty deed, the grantor obligates himself to make the grantee whole if the latter suffers any damage because the grantor's title was defective.

_____11. A mortgagor's right of redemption cannot be extinguished except by operation of law.

Multiple Choice

_____ 1. After a contract of sale is entered into but before the deed has been delivered, the risk of loss or destruction of the property is

a. entirely upon the seller
b. entirely upon the purchaser
c. shared equally by the seller and the purchaser
d. none of the above

_____ 2. A marketable title is one that is free from all of the following except

a. encumberances, suth as mortgages and leases
b. defects in the chain of title appearing in the land records
c. any defects that would subject the purchaser to the inconvenience of having to defend his title in court
d. existing zoning restrictions that are not noted on the deed

_____ 3. Which of the following deeds conveys an after-acquired title to the grantee?

a. a warranty deed
b. a special warranty deed
c. a quitclaim deed
d. none of the above

_____ 4. In order for a deed to be effective, it must be

a. exchanged for consideration
b. delivered
c. recorded
d. all of the above

_____ 5. A State in which an unrecorded deed is invalid against any deed recorded before it is

a a notice State
b. a notice-race State
c. a race State
d. all of the above

_____ 6. Which of the following are elements of a secured transaction?

a. a debt or obligation to pay money
b. an interest of the creditor in specific property which secures performance of the obligation
c. neither (a) nor (b)
d. both (a) and (b)

_____ 7. The mortgagor retains title to the property in

a. a "lien" theory State
b. a "title" theory State
c. neither (a) nor (b)
d. both (a) and (b)

_____ 8. The mortgagor's right to relieve his mortgaged property from the lien of a mortgage by payment of the indebtedness that it secures is called the right of

a. rescission
b. redemption
c. renegotiation
d. renovation

_____ 9. In many States, if a person openly and continuously occupies the land of another for a statutorily prescribed period, that person will gain title to the land by

a. foreclosure
b. redemption
c. eminent domain
d. adverse possession

_____10. Most zoning ordinances provide for the elimination of non-conforming uses

a. when the use is discontinued
b. when a non-conforming structure is destroyed or is substantially damaged
c. when a non-conforming structure has been permitted to exist for the period of its useful life
d. all of the above

_____11. A restrictive covenant is enforceable only if

a. the restriction was intended to benefit the seller of any lot in the tract
b. the restriction appears somewhere in the chain of title to which the land of the person seeking to enforce the covenant is subject
c. neither (a) nor (b)
d. both (a) and (b)

Short Essay

1. What are the two essential documents involved in the transfer of real estate? What must or should each document contain?

2. What are the three types of deeds? How do they differ in effect?

3. Discuss briefly what is necessary to deliver effectively a deed?

4. Discuss what is meant by a restrictive covenant. How is one terminated?

44

TRUSTS AND WILLS

<u>Chapter Outline</u>

I. Trusts

   A. Types of Trusts

      1. Express Trusts
         a. Charitable trusts
         b. Spendthrift trusts
         c. Totten trusts
      2. Implied Trusts
         a. Constructive trusts
         b. Resulting trusts

   B. Creation of Trusts

      1. The Settlor
      2. Subject Matter
      3. The Trustee
         a. Duties of the trustee
         b. Powers of the trustee
         c. Allocation of principal and income
      4. The Beneficiary

   C. Termination of a Trust

II. Decedent's Estate

   A. Wills

      1. Mental Capacity
         a. Testamentary capacity and power

b. Conduct Invalidating a Will

2. Formal Requirements
   a. Writing
   b. Signature
   c. Attestation
3. Revocation
   a. Destruction or alteration
   b. Later will
   c. Operation of law
   d. Renunciation by the surviving spouse
   e. Ademption and abatement of a bequest
4. Special Types of Wills
   a. Nuncupative wills
   b. Holographic wills
   c. Soldiers' and sailors' wills
   d. Conditional wills
   e. Joint and mutual or reciprocal wills
5. Codicil to a Will

B. Intestate Succession

1. Course of Descent
2. Administration of Estates

Definitions

1. Trust
2. Trustee
3. Beneficiary
4. Settlor
5. Express trust
6. Implied trust
7. Constructive trust
8. Resulting trust
9. Charitable trust
10. Spendthrift trust
11. Totten trust
12. Trust corpus
13. Testamentary trust
14. *Inter vivos* trust
15. Ademption
16. Abatement
17. Nuncupative will
18. Holographic will
19. Codicil
20. Intestate succession
21. *Per stirpes*
22. *Per capita*
23. Probate
24. Executor
25. Administrator

True - False

_____ 1. Legal title to property may be held by one or more persons while at the same time its use, enjoyment and benefit belong to one or more others.

_____ 2. An express trust must be in writing in order to be valid.

_____ 3. A constructive trust is created by express language of the settlor, written or oral, by which specific property is transferred to a trustee for the use and benefit of one or more beneficiaries.

_____ 4. A resulting trust is founded on a presumed intent out of the acts of the parties.

_____ 5. Consideration is an essential element of an enforceable trust.

_____ 6. Anyone legally capable of holding title to and dealing with property may be a trustee.

_____ 7. The death of a trustee destroys the trust.

_____ 8. In general, unless the settlor reserves a power of revocation, a trust once validly created is irrevocable.

_____ 9. A will is generally revocable by the testator at any time during his lifetime.

_____10. A will must always be in writing to be effective.

_____11. A holographic will does not need to be witnessed to be valid.

_____12. A codicil must be executed with all of the formal requirements of a will.

_____13. Legally adopted children are generally recognized as lawful heirs of their adopting parents.

Multiple Choice

_____ 1. The party holding legal title to the property in trust is known as

a. the beneficiary
b. the trustee
c. the settlor
d. the creator

_____ 2. If a director of a corporation is found to have taken advantage of a "corporate opportunity", the court will impose

a. an express trust
b. a copnstructive trust
c. a resulting trust
d. a charitable trust

_____ 3. All of the following are correct statements concerning a resulting trust except

a. It serves to carry out the true intent of the parties in those cases where the intent was inadequately expressed
b. It is created by implication and operation of law
c. It is designed to rectify fraud, duress, or a breach of confidence
d. none of the above

_____ 4. A spendthrift clause in a trust instrument will insulate income already received from the trust by the beneficiary from

a. the claims of the beneficiary's creditors
b. the beneficiary's control
c. neither (a) nor (b)
d. both (a) and (b)

_____ 5. A trust created by a settlor's will is

a. a resulting trust
b. a charitable trust
c. a testamentary trust
d. an *inter vivos* trust

_____ 6. Which of the following is not a duty of a trustee?

a. to carry out the purposes of the trust.
b. to act with prudence and care in the administration of the trust
c. to exercise a high degree of loyalty toward the beneficiary
d. to act as a guarantor for the liabilities of the trust

_____ 7. In order to make a valid will, the testator must have

a. the "power" to make a valid will, as defined by state law
b. the "capacity" to make a valid will
c. either (a) or (b)
d. both (a) and (b)

_____ 8. To incorporate by reference a memorandum into a will, all of the following conditions must exist <u>except</u>

a. it must be in writing
b. it must be in existence when the will is executed
c. it must be physically attached to the will
d. it must be adequately described in the will

_____ 9. Which of the following will result in the revocation of a will?

a. The testator is divorced after having executed the will.
b. The testator executes a codicil.
c. The testator marries after having executed the will.
d. The testator tears the will in half thinking that it is a void "I.O.U."

_____10. If A executes a will leaving "Blackacre" to B, but then sells the land for $20,000 before he dies, on A's death, B will receive

a. Blackacre
b. $20,000
c. Green Acre
d. Nothing

Short Essay

1. What are the four essential elements of a trust?

2. Distinguish between a constructive trust and a resulting trust?

3. How is a trust created? How is one terminated?

4. What are the requirements of a valid will? When does it become effective?

5. Outline briefly the steps involved in the adminstration of an estate.

45

INSURANCE

Chapter Outline

A. Kinds of Insurance

1. Life Insurance
   a. Ordinary life
   b. Term life
2. Endowment and Annuity Contracts
3. Accident and Health Insurance
4. Fire Insurance
5. Casualty Insurance
6. Collision insurance
7. Liability insurance
8. No-fault insurance
9. Credit insurance
10. Fidelity insurance
11. Group insurance
12. Marine insurance
13. Title insurance

B. Nature of Insurance Contracts

1. Offer and Acceptance
2. Insurable Interest
   a. Property insurance
   b. Life insurance
3. Premiums
4. Double Indemnity
5. Defenses of the Insurer
   a. Misrepresentations
   b. Breach of Warranty
   c. Concealment

6. Waiver and Estoppel
7. Performance and Termination
    a. Cancellation
    b. Notice

Definitions

1. Insurance
2. Insured
3. Beneficiary
4. Life insurance
5. Whole life insurance
6. Cash surrender value
7. Term life insurance
8. Endowment contract
9. Annuity contract
10. Co-insurance
11. Casualty insurance
12. Collision insurance
13. No-fault insurance
14. Title insurance
15. Insurable interest
16. Double indemnity
17. Incontestability clause

True - False

_____ 1. Insurance is a contractual undertaking.

_____ 2. Insurance is regulated primarily by federal law.

_____ 3. With whole-life insurance, the insured has a right to borrow from the insurer an amount not to exceed the cash surrender value of the policy.

_____ 4. Proceeds from a term life insurance policy will be paid only if the insured dies within the period specified by the policy.

_____ 5. Credit insurance protects debtors against loss due to the insolvency of their creditors.

_____ 6. Title insurance protects property owners against loss arising from defects in the title to real estate, but not against defects due to liens or encumbrances on the property.

_____ 7. An insurance agent's solicitation of a person to purchase an insurance policy usually constitutes an offer by the company to the person that can be accepted by completing the application form.

_____ 8. Property insurance policies are not assignable before loss occurs, but they are freely assignable after the loss.

_____ 9. An insured may not assign the proceeds of his life insurance to a third person who has no insurable interest.

_____10. The principal remedy of the insurer upon discovery of a misrepresentation by the insured is rescission of the contract.

_____11. An "incontestability clause" makes a life insurance policy unassailable by the insurer, even if the insured misreresents his age.

_____12. In order to invalidate an insurance policy, a non-disclosure must generally be both material and fraudulent.

Multiple Choice

_____ 1. The type of life insurance that has a cash surrender value is known as

a. term life insurance
b. ordinary life insurance
c. casualty insurance
d. all of the above

_____ 2. An agrement by an insurer to pay a lump sum of money to the insured when he reaches a certina age or to a beneficiary in the event of premature death is called

a. an annuity contract
b. an endowment contract
c. a life insurance contract
d. none of the above

_____ 3. If a building valued at $20,000 is covered by a $12,000 fire insurance policy with an 80 percent co-insurance clause and the building suffers $10,000 damage by fire, the insurer would pay

a. $3,750
b. $7,500
c. $8,000
d. $10,000

_____ 4. Under a "no-fault" insurance policy, coverage is provided for personal injury to

a. the named insured and passengers in the motor vehicle
b. pedestrians injured by the motor vehicle
c. authorized operators of the motor vehicle
d. all of the above

_____ 5. An insurance contract generally becomes binding upon the insurer when

a. the insurance agent solicits the contract
b. the insured completes the application form and submits it to the insurer
c. when the insurer accepts the application of the insured
d. none of the above

_____ 6. A person does not have an insurable interest in the life of

a. his debtor
b. himself
c. his business parter
d. his neighbor

_____ 7. An insurable interest in property must exist at

a. the time that the insurance contract is entered into
b. the time that the property loss occurs
c. either (a) or (b)
d. both (a) and (b)

_____ 8. An insured may assign the proceeds of a life insurance policy

a. to himself
b. to anyone with an insurable interest in the insured
c. to anyone, including persons with an insurable interest in the insured
d. it may not be assigned prior to loss

_____ 9. A representation by or on behalf of an applicant will have legal consequences if

a. it was relied upon by the insurer as an inducement to enter into a contract
b. it must have been substantially false when made or it must have become so with the insured's knowledge before the contract was created
c. either (a) or (b)
d. both (a) and (b)

_____ 10. An incontestability clause does <u>not</u> prevent the insurer from contesting the policy on which of the following grounds?

a. failure to pay the premiums
b. misrepresentation of age
c. lack of insurable interest by the policy owner
d. all of the above

Short Essay

1. Distinguish between ordinary life insurance and term life insurance.

2. How do endowment contracts and annuity contracts differ from life insurance contracts?

3. Describe briefly the concept of insurable interest. What purpose does it serve.

4. Of what significance are warranties in insurance contracts? How do they operate?

5. Distinguish between waiver and estoppel.

1

INTRODUCTION TO LAW

True - False

1. T
2. F
3. F
4. T
5. T
6. T
7. F
8. F
9. T
10. T
11. T
12. F

Multiple Choice

1. B
2. D
3. D
4. D
5. C
6. A
7. B
8. A
9. D
10. B
11. C

Short Essay

1. In civil law systems, the legislatures create the laws and the judges initiate and conduct the litigation through the inquisitorial method of adjudication. In common law systems, the legislatures, administrative agencies and the judges create the laws, the parties initiate and conduct the litigation through the adversary system, and the judges act as referees to insure that the parties follow the procedural rules.

2. When a court decides a case, not only does it resolve the immediate conflict, but it also indicates to the public how the court is likely to decide similar cases in the future. Thus, people gain a better understanding of their rights and responsibilities and are better able to conform their conduct to the requirements of the law. To the extent that courts do not adhere to their precedents and decide similar cases with different results, people cannot be sure whether they were conforming to the law. This would undermine people's confidence in the law.

3. By administering statutes which apply to specific areas of government control, these expert bodies regulate and supervise complicated areas of the economy that are beyond the effectiveness of the traditional branches of government. Thus, they are intended to insure the orderly flow of commerce, the safety of consumers and workers, and the efficient use of resources.

4. They define the structure of a government, the nature and extent of a government's power, and the rights and liberties of the people. In short, they limit the power of a government to enact laws which restrict the rights and liberties of the people.

2

THE JUDICIAL SYSTEM

<u>True</u> - <u>False</u>

1. T
2. F
3. T
4. F
5. T
6. T
7. T
8. F
9. F
10. F
11. T

<u>Multiple</u> <u>Choice</u>

1. C
2. B
3. C
4. D
5. C
6. B
7. A
8. D
9. C
10. B
11. A

<u>Short</u> <u>Essay</u>

1. An appeal by right is an appeal which the U.S. Supreme Court must hear. Such appeals usually concern the constitutionality of Federal or State statutes. An appeal by writ of certiorari is a discretionary appeal - the Supreme Court has the option to refuse to hear the appeal. Such appeals are more likely to be heard if they concern a federal question of substantial importance or a conflict in the decisions of the U.S. Circuit Courts of Appeals.

2. The judge assumes that all the evidence introduced by the non-moving party is true. He then asks himself whether this evidence, if true, would be sufficient for the jury to find in favor of the non-moving party. If the evidence of the non-moving party, assumed to be true, is not sufficient for the jury to find in favor of the non-moving party, then there is no point in requiring the moving party to try to disprove that evidence. Thus, the moving party will be entitled to a directed verdict.

3. The essential elements are:

    1. the relevant facts
    2. a duty owed by the defendant to the plaintiff
    3. the defendant's breach of that duty
    4. injury to the plaintiff proximately caused by the breach
    5. prayer for relief

3
INTENTIONAL TORTS

True - False

1. F
2. T
3. T
4. F
5. F
6. T
7. T
8. T
9. F
10. F

Multiple Choice

1. C
2. A
3. C
4. B
5. D
6. D
7. A
8. C
9. B
10. D

Short Essay

1. Tresspass is an interference with a person's right to the exclusive possession of his property, while nuisance is an interference with a person's right to use and enjoy his property. Tresspass usually occurs when the wrongdoer attempts to exercise possession of the land by actually coming onto the land. Nuisance, on the other hand, usually occurs when the wrongdoer makes it difficult or impossible for the property owner to use or enjoy his land by subjecting it to such irritants as dust, smoke, noise, or unpleasant odors.

2. For purposes of tort law, a wrongdoer intends to commit a particular tort if he acts with the purpose or motive of achieving the tortious result or with the knowledge that such tortious result is substantially certain to occur as a natural consequence of his actions. For example, if A throws a rock at B, hoping to hit her, he has acted with the purpose of battering her and so he has the requisite intent. If, however, A throws a rock into a large crowd at a rock concert, not hoping to hit anybody at all, he can hardly be surprised when someone is in fact hit. Thus, he will have acted with the knowledge that a battery was substantially certain to occur as a natural consequence of his action and so he would have the requisite intent.

3. In general, one's conduct is privileged if it furthers an interest of such social importance that the harm to an individual is outweighed by the benefit to society. For example, a person may enjoy absolute immunity from liability for defamation even though the defamed individual is harmed because of the overriding public policy which favors complete freedom of speech.

4

NEGLIGENCE AND STRICT LIABILITY

True - False

1. T
2. F
3. F
4. T
5. T
6. F
7. T
8. T
9. F
10. T

Multiple Choice

1. D
2. C
3. B
4. B
5. A
6. C
7. D
8. C
9. C
10. A

Short Essay

1. The reasonable man standard is ordinarily used to determine a defendant's negligence by comparing what the defendant did to what a reasonable man acting prudently and with due care under the circumstances would have done. Some statutes impose a specific standard of care upon certain classes of defendants for the protection of certain classes of plaintiffs. Thus, the courts may take the requirements of a statute as the applicable standard of care in determining the negligence of a particular defendant if the defendant violated a statute which is intended to protect a particular class of persons of which the plaintiff is a member against the particular hazard and kind of harm which resulted.

2. The elements are:
    1. defendant's legal duty
    2. breach of that duty
    3. the breach proximately caused plaintiff's injuries
    4. which are protected against negligent interference

3. A person's actions are a cause in fact of an event whenever the event would not have occurred but for those actions or if those actions were a substantial factor in bringing about the event. A person's actions are the proximate cause of an event whenever the consequences of the event are sufficiently closely related to the actions to hold that person legally responsible for those consequences. Thus, proximate cause tends to limit the liability of a person for the consequences of those events which his actions have in fact caused.

5

INTRODUCTION TO CONTRACTS

True - False

1. F
2. T
3. F
4. F
5. T
6. F
7. T
8. F
9. F
10. T
11. T

Multiple Choice

1. A
2. B
3. D
4. B
5. A
6. D
7. C
8. A
9. C

Short Essay

1. The law of contracts is governed primarily by State common law. An often-cited source of this law is found in the Restatements of the Law of Contracts promulgated by the American Law Institute. The Restatement, Second, of Contracts was adopted by the Institute on May 17, 1979. In all States except Louisiana, however, Article Two of the Uniform Commerical Code governs sales. A sale is a contract involving the transfer of title to movable, tangible personal property from seller to buyer for a price. In all transactions to which Article Two does not apply, and in all those governed by Article Two but where general contract law has not been specifically modified by the Code, contract common law continues to apply.

2. The contract to provide accounting services to X for $15,000 does not depend upon mere formality for its legal validity, and therefore is classified as an <u>informal</u> contract. Moreover, the contract involves an oral manifestation of willingness by both parties to enter into a contract, and therefore it is <u>express</u>, even though not in writing. The contract also involves an exchange of promises - X's promise to provide accounting services for 1 year in exchange for Y's promise to pay $15,000 to X - and therefore is <u>bilateral</u>. There is no evidence that the contract is void, voidable, or otherwise unenforceable. Finally, since, at its inception, neither party has performed any of its duties, the contract is <u>executory</u>.

6

MUTUAL ASSENT

True - False

1. F
2. T
3. F
4. F
5. T
6. T
7. T
8. F
9. F
10. T
11. T
12. T
13. F
14. T
15. F

Multiple Choice

1. D
2. D
3. A
4. C
5. C
6. C
7. D
8. D
9. C
10. B
11. C

Short Essay

1. In order for an offer to have legal effect and thereby confer upon the offeree a power of acceptance (1) it must be communicated to the offeree, (2) it must manifest an intent to enter into a contact, and (3) it must be sufficiently definite and certain in its terms.

   In order to have the mutual assent requisite to the formation of a contract, the offer must be communicated to the offeree by the offeror or by one authorized to do so on the offeror's behalf. Moreover, the offeree must have knowledge of the offer because he cannot agree to something about which he does not know. The offer must also manifest an intent to enter into a contract. Whether a proposal contains such an intent is judged according to an objective, reasonable person standard, rather than according to the subjective intentions of either party. Finally, the offer must be reasonably certain in its terms so as to provide a court with a basis for determining whether a contract actually exists and for giving an appropriate remedy. If the parties intended to form a contract, it will be upheld and missing terms will be supplied by course of dealing, usage of trade, or by inference.

2. An offer may lapse either upon the running of the period of time specified in the offer itself, or if no such time is stated, upon the expiration of a reasonable period of time. The offeror may also revoke his offer at any time prior to acceptance unless the offer is held open by an option

contract, is a merchant's firm offer under the Code, is statutorily irrevocable, or is for a unilateral contract and the offeree has begun the requested performance. An offeree's power of acceptance may also be terminated by the offeree's communicated rejection. The rejection is effective from the moment that it is received by the offeror.

A counter offer or a conditional acceptance both indicate an unwillingness to agree to the terms of the offer and, therefore, operate as a rejection. They are to be distinguished, however, from mere inquiries about the possibility of obtaining new or different terms for the contract, as these do not terminate the offer. Finally, an offer will be terminated by the death or insanity of the offeror or of the offeree, or by the destruction of the specific subject matter of the contract, or if performance of the previously valid offer is subsequently made illegal.

3. Under the common law "mirror image" rule, an acceptance must be positive and unequivocal. It may not change any of the terms of the offer, nor add to, subtract from, or otherwise qualify the terms of the offer in any way. Any communication that attempts to do so is not an acceptance but rather is a mere counter-offer.

   In contrast, the Code modifies this rule to account for the realities of modern business practices, the most notable being the extensive use of the standardized business form. The Code focuses on the intent of the parties; if the offeree definitely and reasonably expresses his acceptance of the offer and does not expressly make his acceptance conditional on the buyer's assent to the additional or different terms, then a contract is formed. Here the issue becomes whether the seller's different or additional terms become part of the contract. The Code provides rules to resolve these disputes depending on whether the parties are merchants and on whether the terms are additional or different terms.

7

CONDUCT INVALIDATING ASSENT

True - False

1. T
2. F
3. F
4. T
5. F
6. F
7. T
8. F
9. T
10. F
11. T
12. T
13. T

Multiple Choice

1. A
2. C
3. C
4. D
5. C
6. D
7. D
8. B
9. A
10. B

Short Essay

1. There are two basic types of duress: The first occurs when a party is compelled to assent to a contract through physical force. This form of duress renders the purported agreement void.

   The second type of duress involves the use of improper threats to compel a person to enter into a contract. The threat may be explicit or inferred from words or conduct. A subjective test is used to determine whether the threat actually induced assent on the part of the person claiming to be the victim of duress. Duress of this kind renders the resulting contract voidable at the option of the coerced.

2. The two types of fraud are fraud in the execution and fraud in the inducement. Fraud in the execution consists of a representation as to the very nature of the contract being entered into. The resulting contract is void because assent was not knowingly given.

   The second type of fraud is fraud in the inducement. It occurs when there is a misrepresentation of material fact made by one party to the contract to the other who in turn consents to enter into the contract in reliance upon that misrepresentation. To establish fraud of this type, one must show that the other party made a false representation of a fact that is material, that it was made with knowledge of its falsity and the intention to deceive, and that the misrepresentation was justifiably relied upon. The resulting agreement is voidable at the election of the defrauded party again because his assent was not knowingly given.

3. The contract is voidable due to mutual mistake of fact. The contract here entered into was based upon a mutual mistake of material fact.

8
CONSIDERATION

True - False

1. F
2. F
3. F
4. F
5. T
6. T
7. F
8. T
9. T
10. F
11. T

Multiple Choice

1. D
2. C
3. A
4. B
5. D
6. B
7. D
8. B
9. B
10. A

Short Essay

1. Mutuality of consideration means that the promises or performance of both parties to a contract must be legally sufficient for the contract to be enforceable by either. To be legally sufficient, a promise or performance must be either a legal benefit to the promisor or a legal detriment to the promisee. In this regard, legal benefit means the obtaining by the promisor of that which he had no legal right to obtain. A legal detriment means the doing of that which the promisor was under no prior legal obligation to do, or the refraining from doing that which he was previously under no legal obligation to refrain from doing.

2. The two essential elements of consideration are (1) legal sufficiency (value) and (2) bargained-for exchange. In short, consideration is a bargained-for exchange of value. The adequacy of consideration, however, is irrelevant and the subject matter that the parties respectively have exchanged need not have approximate value. Rather, the law will treat the parties as having considered the subject of the exchange adequate by reason of their having freely agreed to the exhange.

3. Illusory promises are not enforceable because their performance is entirely optional in the discretion of the promisor. As such, the promisor suffers no legal detriment by his promise nor does he confer legal benefit. In short, an illusory promise is not legally sufficient.

   Output and requirements contracts differ from illusory promises in that the promisor agrees to sell all of his output or to purchase all of his supplies of a particular kind rather than to sell or to buy as much as he desires. Moreover, the Code imposes an obligation of good faith on requirements and output contracts to insure against an unfair result.

9

ILLEGAL BARGAINS

True - False

1. T
2. F
3. T
4. F
5. F
6. F
7. F
8. T
9. T

Multiple Choice

1. D
2. B
3. A
4. C
5. B
6. B
7. D
8. C
9. D

Short Essay

1. An essential requirement of a binding promise or agreement is legality of objective. Thus, a contract, by definition, is a legal and enforceable agreement. Illegal agreements are not enforceable in order (1) to discourage such undesirable conduct in the future, and (2) to avoid the inappropriate use of the judicial process in carrying out the socially undesirable bargain.

2. The two types of licensing statutes are those which are regulatory in nature and those enacted in order to raise revenue. A regulatory licensing statute is one designed to protect the public against services provided by unqualified individuals. If violated, there can be no recovery for professional services rendered by a person not having the required license.

   A revenue-raising licensing statute is one designed solely to raise revenue, and does not seek to protect the public from services provided by incompetents. Accordingly, agreements by persons not having the license required by such a statute are enforceable.

10

CONTRACTUAL CAPACITY

True - False

1. F
2. T
3. F
4. T
5. T
6. F
7. T
8. T
9. F
10. F
11. F
12. T

Multiple Choice

1. D
2. B
3. A
4. C
5. B
6. D
7. D
8. B
9. D

Short Essay

1. Necessaries are generally regarded as those things needed by a person to maintain his particular station in life. Obviously included, therefore, are those items necessary for subsistence and health, such as food, lodging, clothing, and medical services. Other items essential to a person's ability to earn a livelihood may also be included.

2. If a minor disaffirms a contract, most states require only that the minor return any property that he has received from the other party provided it is in the minor's possession at the time of disaffirmance. If an incompetent disaffirms a contract, however, the duty is somewhat different. If the contract is fair and if the competent party had no reason to suspect the other's incompetency, the incompetent must restore the competent party to its status quo by a return of the consideration received or its equivalent in money. Finally, with regard to intoxicated persons, the courts enforce the requirement of restitution even more strictly than with regard to incompetents.

11

CONTRACTS IN WRITING

True - False

1. F
2. T
3. T
4. F
5. F
6. F
7. T
8. T
9. F
10. F

Multiple Choice

1. C
2. B
3. D
4. B
5. B
6. D
7. C
8. D
9. B
10. C

Short Essay

1. An original promise, which is within the Statute of Frauds, is one in which the primisor himself is primarily liable. A collateral promise, by contrast, is one in which the promisor is secondarily liable.

2. As a general rule, a promise to transfer an interest in land is within the Statute of Frauds and therefore must comply with its requirements. There are two exceptions to that rule however. The first involves a promise to make a short term lease. In most states this is defined by statute to include leases that are for one year or less in duration. The second involves an oral contract that may be enforced if the party seeking enforcement has so changed his position in reasonable reliance upon the contract that injustice can only be prevented by enforcing the contract.

3. The general contract Statute of Frauds requires that an agreement be in writing to be enforceable. The writing has to be signed by the party to be charged or his agent; specify the parties to the contract; and specify with reasonable certainty the subject matter and the essential terms of the unperformed promises. The Statute of Frauds provision under the U.C.C. is more liberal. The Code requires only a writing that is sufficient to indicate that a contract has been made between the parties; signed by the party against whom enforcement is sought or by his authorized agent; and specify the quantity of goods to be sold. An oral contract for the sale of goods may comply with the requirements of the Code in the following four instances: (1) where written confirmation of a contract between merchants is sent and no objection is made within 10 days; (2) where the party defending against the contract admits it by pleading, testimony, or otherwise in court; (3) under certain

circumstances, where the goods are to be specially manufactured; and (4) where there has been payment or delivery and acceptance.

4. The parol evidence rule does not apply in the following six situations.

   1. Where the contract is partly written and partly oral.
   2. Where there is a clerical or typographical error which obviously does not represent the agreement of the parties.
   3. Where there is a lack of contractual capacity on the part of one of the parties.
   4. Where there is a defense asserted of fraud, duress, undue influence, mistake or illegality.
   5. A condition precedent agreed upon and to which the entire agreement was made subject.
   6. A subsequent mutual rescission or modification of the written contract.

12

RIGHTS OF THIRD PARTIES

True - False

1. T
2. F
3. T
4. F
5. F
6. T
7. T
8. T
9. T
10. F
11. T

Multiple Choice

1. A
2. C
3. D
4. A
5. D
6. B
7. D
8. C
9. A
10. C

Short Essay

1. An assignment of rights is the voluntary transfer to a third party (the assignee) of the rights arising from a contract. A delegation of duties, on the other hand, is a transfer to a third party (the delegatee) of the contractual duty to perform. An effective assignment extinguishes the assignor's right of performance by the obligor. Therefore, only the assignee has a right to the obligor's performance. A delegation of duty, however, does not extinguish the delegator's duty to perform, but only results in an additional party, the delegatee, also being obligated.

2. Notice to the obligor is not a precondition to a valid assignment. Nevertheless, notice of the assignment should be given because in its absence an assignee will lose his rights against the obligor if the latter pays the assignor without notice of the assignment. Moreover, the obligor's set off's and counterclaims against the assignor that arise out of separate transactions and after notice has been given cannot be used against the assignee.

3. The majority American rule regarding the successive assignment of the same contractual rights provides that a prior assignee is entitled to the assigned right and its proceeds to the exclusion of a subsequent assignee. The rule, however, does not apply where the prior assignment is revocable or voidable by the assignor. It also does not apply where the subsequent assignee in good faith and without knowledge of the prior assignment gives value and obtains payment or satisfaction of the obligor's duty; obtains a judgment against the obligor; obtains a novation with the obligor; or

obtains possession of a writing of a type customarily accepted as a symbol or as evidence of the right assigned.

4. An intended creditor beneficiary is a third person to whom the promisee owes a legal duty that the performance of the promise is intended to satisfy. An intended gratuitous (or donee) beneficiary, on the other hand is a third party to whom the promisee intends to make a gift by way of the performance of a bargained-for promise by the promisor. While an intended gratuitous beneficiary only has rights against the promisor, an intended creditor beneficiary has rights against the promisee based upon the original obligation and against the promisor based on the third party beneficiary contract.

13

PERFORMANCE, BREACH AND DISCHARGE

True - False

1. T	6. F
2. F	7. T
3. T	8. F
4. F	9. T
5. T	10. F

Multiple Choice

1. B	7. D
2. C	8. B
3. D	9. C
4. C	10. C
5. A	11. B
6. B	

Short Essay

1. There is an important difference between the effect of the breach or non-performance of a contract and the effect of the failure or non-occurrence of a condition. A breach of contract, on the one hand, subjects the promisor to liability. Moreover, depending upon its materiality, the breach may excuse the promisee for non-performance of his duty under the contract. The occurrence or non-occurrence of a condition, on the other hand, either prevents the promisee from acquiring a right or deprives him of a right. It does not, however, subject either party to liability.

2. At common law, a party was discharged from his duty to perform under the contract on grounds of impossibility only if it was objectively impossible for anyone to preform. The courts also generally regarded frustration of purpose as a discharge where the purpose of the contract was frustrated by fortuitous circumstances that deprived the performance of the value attached to it by the parties. The Restatement and the Code positions, however, are that literal impossibility is not required, and that commercial impracticability resulting from a supervening event will excuse non-performance. The supervening event, however, must have been a "basic assumption" that both parties made when they entered into the contract.

14
REMEDIES

True - False

1. T	8. F
2. F	9. T
3. F	10. F
4. F	11. T
5. T	12. F
6. F	13. T
7. T	

Multiple Choice

1. A	6. A
2. D	7. D
3. B	8. D
4. C	9. A
5. C	10. A

Short Essay

1. Damages are only recoverable for a loss resulting from a breach of contract to the extent that the party in breach had reason to foresee that such loss would be a probable result of such a breach when the parties entered into the contract. The test of foreseeability is an objective one based upon what the breaching party had reason to foresee. A foreseeable loss is one which follows a breach in the ordinary course of events, or from special circustances of which the party in breach either knew or had reason to know.

2. Under the doctrine of mitigation of damages the party injured by a breach of contract must take such steps as may be reasonably calculated to lessen the damages that he may sustain. Damages are not recoverable for losses that the injured party could have avoided without undue risk, burden or humiliation.

3. The two major equitable remedies applicable to a breach of contract are the decree of specific performance and the injunction. A decree of specific performance orders a breaching party to render the performance promised under the contract. In contrast, an injunction is an order issued by a court of equity commanding a person to refrain from doing a specific act or engaging in specified conduct. Gnerally, both are available only where damages for a breach would be inadequate. However, a court will not decree specific performance of a contract for personal services. Nor will it issue an injunction to enforce an exclusive

personal service contract if the probable result would be to leave the employee without other reasonable means of making a living.

4. Restitution is a return to the aggrieved party of the consideration, or its value, that he gave to the other party. It is available as a remedy in several contractual situations: (1) as an alternative remedy for a breach of contract; (2) for a party in default; (3) for a party who may not enforce a contract because of the Statute of Frauds; and (4) upon the avoidance of a voidable contract.

15
INTRODUCTION TO SALES

True - False

1.	T	6.	T
2.	T	7.	F
3.	F	8.	F
4.	F	9.	T
5.	T	10.	T

Multiple Choice

1.	B	6.	B
2.	A	7.	B
3.	D	8.	B
4.	D	9.	D
5.	C	10.	A

Short Essay

1. Article Two of the Uniform Commercial Code is expressly applicable to contracts for the sale of goods, as it defines those terms. General contract law, however, continues to govern aspects of the sale of goods not specifically modified by the Code as well as contracts outside the scope of the Code. These include transactions other than sales, such as bailments, leases and gifts, as well as sales of things other than goods, such as services, real property, and intangibles. Nevertheless, the Code is often applied by analogy to non-sales transactions, thereby expanding the scope of its principles and policies.

2. At common law, the "mirror-image" rule required that an acceptance not vary from the terms of the offer. The Code, in contrast, has taken a more liberal approach necessitated by the realities of modern business practices, most notably the standardized business form utilized in most commercial transactions. Accordingly, the Code provides that unless the language in the offer or the surrounding circumstances clearly indicate otherwise, an offer to make a contract invites acceptance in any manner and by any medium reasonable in the circumstances.

3. All transactions within the scope of the Code are subject to a requirement of "good-faith" which is defined as "honesty in fact in the conduct or transaction concerned." In addition, in the case of a merchant, the "good faith" standard requires that the merchant observe "reasonable commercial standards of fair dealing in the trade." The first standard is a subjective one, focusing as it does on the motives of the parties involved. The second, however, is an objective standard by which the merchant is held to a standard considered fair in the trade.

16

TRANSFER OF TITLE AND RISK OF LOSS

True - False

1. T
2. F
3. F
4. T
5. T
6. F
7. F
8. T
9. F
10. F
11. F
12. T
13. T
14. F
15. F
16. T

Multiple Choice

1. B
2. D
3. A
4. B
5. B
6. B
7. D
8. C
9. D
10. C
11. C
12. D

Short Essay

1. At common law, risk of loss was placed upon the party that had title to the goods at the time in question. The Code, however, employs a transactional approach that diminishes the importance of the concept of title. Accordingly, the Code sets forth a detailed set of rules for allocating risk of loss depending on whether there has been a breach of the sales contract. In the absence of a breach, the Code attempts to place the risk of loss upon the party who is more likely to have greater control over the goods or is better able to prevent the loss.

2. A shipment contract is one that authorizes the seller to send the goods to the buyer but does not require the seller to deliver the goods to a particular destination. A destination contract, by contrast, requires the seller to deliver the goods to a particular destination. Under the former, title and risk of loss pass to the buyer at the time and place that the seller delivers the goods to the carrier; under the latter, title and risk of loss pass to the buyer upon tender of the goods to him at that destination.

3. A void title to goods is not title and therefore the holder of void title cannot transfer any interest in the goods. A voidable title is one acquired under circumstances that permit the former owner to transfer and revest himself with title. A holder of voidable title has the power to resell the goods to a <u>bona fide</u> purchaser for value and without notice of

any infirmity in the title. If such a subsequent sale takes place, the original seller's right of rescission is cut off and the subsequent <u>bona fide</u> purchaser acquires good title.

4. If goods are held by a bailee and are to be delivered without being moved, risk of loss passes to the buyer on his receipt of a negotiable document of title if one is involved in the transaction. If, however, a non-negotiable document of title is utilized by the bailee as a receipt for the seller's goods being stored, risk of loss passes to the buyer upon tender to him of the document, unless he reasonably objects. If not documents of title are involved risk of loss passes upon either (a) the delivery by the seller to the bailee of a writing that directs the bailee to transfer the goods to the buyer, or (b) an acknowledgment by the bailee of the buyer's right to possession of the goods.

17

PERFORMANCE

True - False

1. T	7. T
2. F	8. T
3. T	9. T
4. F	10. F
5. F	11. T
6. F	

Multiple Choice

1. C	7. A
2. C	8. B
3. C	9. D
4. B	10. D
5. D	11. A
6. C	12. D

Short Essay

1. The seller's basic performance obligation is to tender delivery of conforming goods to the buyer. He is required to put and to hold goods that conform to the contract at the buyer's disposition and to give the buyer notification reasonably necessary to enable her to take delivery.

   The buyer has two basic performance obligations: to accept conforming goods tendered by the seller, and to pay for them according to the terms of the contract. Unless the parties otherwise agree, tender of payment or payment by the buyer is a condition to the seller's duty to tender and to complete any deliver.

2. Unless the parties otherwise agree, the place for delivery of goods is the seller's place of business. Under a shipment contract, however, the seller is obligated to send the goods to the buyer (although he is not required to deliver them to a particular place as in a destination contract). Discharge of his duty of performance under a shipment contract requires the seller to: (1) deliver the goods to a carrier; (2) make a reasonable contract for their shipment; (3) obtain and promptly deliver or tender to the buyer any documents necessary to allow the buyer to obtrain possession of the goods from the carrier; and (4) promptly notify the buyer of the shipment.

3. The doctrine of "cure" is a modification of the buyer's right to reject goods upon the seller's failure to comply with the perfect tender rule. When the buyer refuses to accept a non-conforming tender of goods, the

seller may, by acting promptly and within the time allowed for performance, make a proper tender or delivery of conforming goods and thereby cure his defective tender or performance. Secondly, the Code allows the seller to cure a non-conforming tender that he had reasonble grounds to believe would be acceptable with or without money allowance. If the buyer rejects non-conforming goods without disclosing the existence of a curable defect to the seller, or if he refuses to accept the seller's attempted cure, the buyer may not assert the defect as an excuse for not accepting the goods or as a breach of contract by the seller if the defect is one that is curable.

4. A rejection is a manifestation by the buyer of his unwillingness to become owner of the goods. To be effective, it must be made within a reasonable time after the goods have been tendered or delivered an the seller must be reasonably notified. A buyer may rightfully reject goods that do not conform to the contract, but any exercise of ownership of the goods by the buyer after rejection is wrongful as against the seller. Finally, a buyer's duty after rejection varies depending on whether or not he is a merchant.

   A revocation of acceptance is a manifestation of unwillingness to remain the owner of the goods after the buyer has already accepted them. A buyer may revoke his acceptance of non-conforming goods only if the non-conformity substantially impairs the value of the goods and the acceptance was a) based on the reasonable assumption that the seller would cure the non-conformity and did not, or b) without discovery of the non-conformity and such acceptance was reasonably induced by the difficulty of discovery before acceptance or by assurances of the seller. Upon revocation of acceptance, the buyer is in the same position with respect to the goods and has the same rights and duties with regard to them as if he had rejected them.

5. The parties to a contract can be relieved of their obligations of full performance in three instances. The first is if there has been a loss of goods that were identified when the contract was made, and the loss occurred without the fault of either party and before risk of loss passed to the buyer. If the loss was total, the contract is avoided; if partial, it is voidable at the election of the buyer.

   The second instance is upon the non-happening of a pre-supposed condition that was a basic assumption of the contract. The parties are relieved from their obligation of performance, however, only to the extent of the non-happening of the condition.

   Finally, where neither party is at fault and the agreed manner of delivery of the goods becomes commercially impracticable, a substituted performance, if commercially reasonable, can be tendered by the seller and accepted by the buyer.

18
WARRANTIES AND PRODUCTS LIABILITY

True - False

1. T
2. F
3. F
4. T
5. F
6. F
7. T
8. F
9. F
10. T
11. T
12. F

Multiple Choice

1. B
2. C
3. D
4. B
5. D
6. D
7. A
8. C
9. C
10. A

Short Essay

1. As a general rule under the Code, a seller's opinion of the goods he sells does not create a warranty. Two exceptions to this rule, however, are: (a) if the seller is an expert and gives his opinion as such, he may be liable and (b) if an ordinary seller misrepresents his opinion.

2. Under the implied warranty of merchantability, a merchant seller impledly warrants that the goods that are of the kind in which he deals are merchantable - i.e., that they are reasonably fit for the general purpose for which they are manufactured and sold, and also that they are of fair, average, and merchantable quality. The warranty may apply to second hand goods, and it can be disclaimed, unless barred by the Magnuson-Moss Act, by a conspicuous writing containing language that specially includes merchantability or a similar oral disclaimer.

   Under the implied warranty of fitness for a particular purpose, any seller, whether a merchant or a non-merchant, impliedly warrants that the goods are reasonably fit for the particular purpose of the buyer for which the goods are required provided at the time of contracting the seller has reason to know such particular purpose and that the buyer is relying upon the seller's skill and judgment to furnish suitable goods. The disclaimer of an implied warranty of fitness for the particular purpose must be in writing and conspicuous.

3. In order to recover under a theory of strict liability in tort, a seller must show that: (1) the defendent sold the product in a defective condition; (2) the defendant was engaged in the business of selling such a

product; (3) the defective condition was one that made the product unreasonbly dangerous to the user or consumer or to his property; (4) that the defect in the product existed at the time it left the hands of the defendant; (5) the plantiff sustained physical harm or property damage by use or consumption of the product; and (6) the defective condition was the proximate cause of such injury or damage.

Many of the traditional obstacles to recovery are not applicable to a claim of strict liability in tort. Liability cannot generally be modified or disclaimed, and there is no requirement of horizaontal or vertical privity. Moreover, contributory negligence is, for the most part, not recognized as a valid defense; comparative negligence, however, has on occasion been applied to limit a plaintiff's recovery to account for his degree of fault. Finally, voluntary assumption of the risk is a valid defense to an action based on strict liability in tort.

19

REMEDIES

True - False

1. T
2. F
3. F
4. T
5. T
6. F
7. T
8. T
9. F
10. T
11. F

Multiple Choice

1. C
2. B
3. D
4. C
5. A
6. B
7. D
8. A
9. A
10. D
11. C
12. C
13. B

Short Essay

1. If a buyer has rightfully rejected the seller's non-conforming tender of goods, the buyer has several non-exclusive remedies for the seller's contract breach. First, the buyer may cancel the contract. He may also recover any payments already made, and establish a security interest in any of the seller's goods that are already in his possession to the extent of any payment of the price already made. Finally, he may also cover and recover damages or simply seek market price damages for the seller's breach.

2. All of the remedies outlined in question one are available to a buyer if the seller repudiates a contract, and several more are also available. First, the buyer may maintain an action for replevin of goods that have been identified to the contract if the buyer after a reasonable effort is unable to effect cover for such goods, or if the goods have been shipped under reservation of a security interest in the seller and satisfaction of this security interest has been made or tendered. In addition, if the goods are unique or if money damages would not be an adequate remedy, the buyer may seek specific performance.

3. Several remedies are available to the seller after the buyer has wrongfully rejected a conforming tender of goods. First, the seller may cancel the contract. He may also withhold delivery of additional goods and identify goods to the contract. He may resell and recover damages or

just recover market price damages. Finally, if appropriate, a seller may bring an action for price - this is most likely to occur if conforming goods have been lost or damaged after the risk of loss has passed to the buyer, or where goods have been identified to the contract and there is no ready market available for their resale at a reasonable price.

4. A contract may contain a liquidated damages clause. It will be upheld if the amount specified is reasonable and commensurate with the actual or anticipated loss resulting from the breach. A provision in a contract fixing an unreasonably large liquidated damages amount is void as a penalty. A contract may also limit remedies in the event of breach as long as it is not done in an unconscionable manner, and may even provide for an exclusive remedy. Where circumstances cause an exclusive or limited remedy to fail of its essential purpose, resort may be had to the remedies provided by the Code.

20

FORM AND CONTENT

True - False

1.	T	6.	T
2.	F	7.	T
3.	T	8.	T
4.	F	9.	T
5.	F	10.	F

Multiple Choice

1.	B	6.	C
2.	A	7.	A
3.	D	8.	C
4.	D	9.	D
5.	B	10.	B

Short Essay

1. By postdating it.

2. It is non-negotiable because it is not payable to order or to bearer.

3. The requirement of negotiability are:
    1. The instrument must be in writing
    2. The instrument must be signed
    3. The instrument must contain a promise or order to pay
    4. The instrument must be unconditional
    5. The instrument must be for a sum certain in money
    6. The instrument must contain no other promise or order
    7. The instrument must be payable on demand or at a definite time
    8. The instrument must be payable to order or to bearer

21

TRANSFER

True - False

1. F	6. F
2. T	7. T
3. T	8. F
4. F	9. T
5. T	10. F

Multiple Choice

1. C	6. B
2. B	7. D
3. A	8. C
4. D	9. B
5. C	10. A

Short Essay

1. Not if you are worried about its being lost or stolen. Remember that bearer paper runs to whoever is in possession of it, so that a finder or thief is entitled to payment. On the other hand, if an order instrument such as a check is lost or stolen, the finder or theif is not a holder and is thus not entitled to payment.

2. (1) Blank - merely the indorser's signature makes the instrument bearer paper
   (2) Special - designates the person to whose order the instrument is payable
   (3) Restrictive - attempts to restrict the rights of the indorsee in some fashion (four different types)
   (4) Unrestrictive - without restriction
   (5) Qualified - disclaimer of liability on the contract of indorsement
   (6) Unqualified - guarantee payment if certain conditions are met

22

HOLDER IN DUE COURSE

True - False

1. T
2. T
3. F
4. T
5. T
6. F
7. T
8. F
9. T
10. F

Multiple Choice

1. A
2. D
3. C
4. A
5. B
6. C
7. D
8. A
9. B
10. C

Short Essay

1. Anyone who meets the following requirements may be a holder in due course.
    1. A holder who takes the instrument
    2. for value
    3. in good faith and
    4. without notice that there is anything "wrong" with it

2. A mere holder is nothing more than an assignee. Thus, he takes the rights his transferor had and is subject to the claims and defenses that could be asserted against his transferor. A holder in due course, on the other hand, takes the instrument free from any claims and free from most defenses. Thus, a holder in due course will be entitled to payment in many cases where a mere holder would not be.

3. A holder in due course takes an instrument free from defenses only with respect to parties with whom he has not dealt.

4. In general, when an instrument is incomplete, it may be completed in accordance with the authority given and is then valid and effective as completed. Even the signature may be made by an authorized agent, but you may have a hard time proving to your local merchant that you have authority to sign someone else's checks. The signature notwithstanding, you could legally spend the check by filling in the date, the payee, and the amount of the purchase when your roommate's items have been totalled at the cash register.

23

LIABILITY OF PARTIES

True - False

1. F
2. T
3. F
4. F
5. F
6. F
7. T
8. T
9. T
10. T
11. T

Multiple Choice

1. D
2. D
3. C
4. D
5. D
6. D
7. B
8. B
9. C
10. A
11. A

Short Essay

1. Yes, when the forgery is that of an indorser's signature (under the presenter's warranty as well as possibly under the imposter or fictitious payee rule), or the drawer's signature if the forgery was due to the drawer's negligence. The drawee can also recover under the presenter's warranty for material alteration of the instrument and against the drawer if the material alteration was due to the drawer's negligence.

2. A drawer is only relieved of liability to the extent of any loss suffered by reason of the delay.

3. Under primary liability one is absolutely and unconditionally liable, while under secondary liability one is only liable upon the happening of certain specified events.

4. A drawee is not liable on an insturment. Upon acceptance, a drawee becomes primarily liable under its acceptor's lability.

24

BANK DEPOSITS AND COLLECTIONS

True - False

1. T
2. F
3. F
4. F
5. T
6. T
7. F
8. T
9. F
10. T

Multiple Choice

1. C
2. D
3. B
4. A
5. C
6. A
7. D
8. C
9. C
10. A

Short Essay

1. In general, if you do not indorse your check by the time you deposit it, your bank may indorse it for you.

2. The drawer of a check is secondarily liable on the check, so that a holder may sue the drawer for the amount of the check if the drawee refuses to pay it. Normally, the drawer stops payment in the first place because of a claim or defense against the payee. Such a defense would be valid against the payee or a mere holder, but would not prevent a subsequent holder in due course from obtaining payment.

25

Agency and Employment Relationship

TRUE - FALSE

1. F
2. F
3. T
4. T
5. T
6. T
7. F
8. F
9. T
10. F

Multiple Choice

1. C
2. B
3. D
4. D
5. D
6. B
7. C
8. A
9. C
10. D

Short Essay

1. A fiduciary duty arises when one person is entitled to place his trust and confidence in another. Because of this relationship, the agent does not deal with his principal at arm's length. Thus, the agent owes his principal at all times the duties of loyalty, good faith, and full disclosure.

2. An agent may not (a) represent his principal in any transaction in which he has a personal interest; (b) take a position in conflict with the interests of his principal; (c) compete with his principal; (d) act on behalf of a competitor or for persons whose interests conflict with those of the principal; (e) use for his own benefit, and contrary to the interests of his principal, information obtained in the course of the agency; or (f) make a secret profit out of the subject matter of the agency.

3. The basic defenses are:
   (a) A bona fide seniority system
   (b) A bona fide merit system
   (c) A bona fide occupational qualification
   (d) A professionally developed ability test
   (e) A system based on quantity or quality of production
   (f) Any reasonable system which does not discriminate on a prohibited basis

4. The remedies are:
   (a) Recovery of back pay
   (b) Injunctive relief
   (c) Affirmative action
   (d) Reinstatement

26

RELATIONSHIP WITH THIRD PARTIES

True - False

1. T
2. T
3. T
4. T
5. F
6. F
7. T
8. F
9. T
10. F

Multiple Choice

1. D
2. C
3. C
4. D
5. C
6. B
7. C
8. A
9. A
10. C

Short Essay

1. Actual authority is based upon words or conduct of the principal manifested to the agent. Apparent authority is based upon words or conduct of the principal which manifests to a third person that the agent has actual authority. Actual authority gives an agent both the power and the right to bind his principal in legal relations with third persons, while apparent authority gives the agent the power but not necessarily the right to bind his principal.

2. An agent has the power to bind her principal when the principal is legally bound by the act of the agent. An agent has the right to bind her principal whenever she may do so without violating her duty of obedience by exceeding her actual authority. For example, when an agent has apparent authority but not actual authority she has the power but not the right to bind her principal. Thus, the principal is legally bound by the act of the agent, but by exceeding her actual authority the agent has violated her duty of obedience and is liable to the principal for any resulting loss.

3. The obvious answer is that the employer is liable for the torts of his employee, provided, of course, that at the time of the wrongful act the employee was acting within the scope of his employment.

   The rationale of respondeat superior, however, is to make the employer's vicarious libility the price which the employer must pay for the privilege of enlarging the scope of his business activities through the use of employees. In short, the emloyer is supposed to treat his vicarious liability as just another business expense which is added to the cost of his products. Thus, the people who end up buying his products, through the higher prices they must pay, are the ones who ultimately bear the loss of the employee's negligence.

27

NATURE AND FORMATION

True - False

1. T
2. T
3. F
4. F
5. F
6. T
7. F
8. T
9. F
10. T

Multiple Choice

1. D
2. B
3. D
4. A
5. D
6. C
7. B
8. D
9. D
10. D

Short Essay

1. The court will look for a community of interest for business purposes. Specifically, the court will determine whether there exists
   1. A business
      (a) An intention to acquire profits
      (b) A continuous series of commercial activities
   2. Co-ownership
      (a) A community interest in the capital employed in the business
      (b) A sharing of profits and losses
      (c) A community of authority to conduct the business activities

2. When times are good and the business is making money, an employee may want to prove that he is a partner so that he may share in the profits. On the other hand, when times are bad and the business is losing money, creditors may want to prove that an employee or an investor is a parter and thus liable for the debts of the partnership.

3. A partnership is recognized as a legal entity in certain respects, but as an aggregation of individuals in others. For example, a partnership is considered an entity in that: (a) every partner is considered its agent; (b) its assets, liabilities, and business transactions are considered separate from those of its partners; (c) it may hold title to real estate, sue, and be sued in its own name. On the other hand, a partnership is considered an aggregation in that : (a) its existence is tied to the continued participation of its partners; (b) its debts are ultimately the debts of its partners; (c) its income is taxed to the individual partners.

28

RIGHTS AND DUTIES

True - False

1. T
2. F
3. T
4. T
5. F
6. T
7. F
8. F
9. T
10. T

Multiple Choice

1. D
2. C
3. D
4. D
5. B
6. C
7. B
8. B
9. A
10. B

Short Essay

1. Partners may by agreement vary their legal rights and obligations so long as the rights of third parties are not affected and standards of fairness among the partners are maintained.

2. Partners may agree to
   (a) share profits and losses unequally
   (b) pay interest on capital contributions
   (c) pay salaries to one or more of the partners
   (d) share management responsibilities unequally
   (e) keep the books of the partnership somewhere other than the principal place of business and to limit partners' access to them

3. A partner has actual implied authority to
   (a) hire and fire employees whose services are necessary to carry on the business of the partnership
   (b) purchase property necessary for the business
   (c) make repairs reasonably necessary for the proper conduct of the business
   (d) make contracts which are incidental to the business
   (e) sell goods in accordance with the purposes for which the business is operated
   (f) receive payment of sums due the partnership
   (g) pay debts due from the partnership arising out of the business enterprise
   (h) direct the ordinary operations of the business

29

DISSOLUTION AND TERMINATION

True - False

1. T
2. T
3. F
4. F
5. F
6. F
7. F
8. F
9. T
10. T
11. T

Multiple Choice

1. B
2. C
3. A
4. C
5. C
6. D
7. A
8. C
9. D
10. B

Short Essay

1. Winding up a partnership involves
   (a) completing unfinished business
   (b) collecting receivables
   (c) reducing assets to cash
   (d) taking inventory
   (e) auditing the partnership books
   (f) paying creditors
   (g) distributing the remaining assets to the partners

2. Dissolution may be brought about by
   (a) an act of the parties
   (b) operation of law
   (c) court order

3. The order of distribution of an insolvent partner's assets is
   (a) debts and liabilities owing to non-partnership creditors
   (b) debts and liabilities owing to partnership creditors
   (c) contributions owing to other partners by reason of payments by them to partnership creditors in excess of their respective share of the liabilities of the firm

4. The order of distribution of a general partnership's assets is
   (a) to creditors other than partners
   (b) to partners other than for capital and profits
   (c) to partners in respect of capital
   (d) to partners in respect of profits

30

LIMITED PARTNERSHIPS

True - False

1. T
2. F
3. T
4. F
5. T
6. F
7. T
8. F
9. T
10. F
11. F

Multiple Choice

1. D
2. A
3. B
4. C
5. D
6. B
7. C
8. B
9. D
10. D

Short Essay

1. A limited partner may rightfully demand the return of his contibution upon
   (a) dissolution of the partnership
   (b) the date specified in the certificate for its return
   (c) six months' written demand if no time is specified in the certificate for the return of the contribution or for dissolution

2. A limited partner is protected against unlimited personal liability only if the following conditions are met:
   (a) there is substantial compliance in good faith with the requirement that a certificate of limited partnership be filed
   (b) the surname of the limited partner does not appear in the partnership name
   (c) the limited partner does not take part in control of the business

3. A limited partnership is dissolved
   (a) at the time, or upon the happening of the events, specified in the certificate
   (b) upon the unanimous written consent of all the parties
   (c) upon the withdrawal of a general partner
   (d) by a decree of judicial dissolution

4. (a) fiduciary duty
   (b) duty of obedience
   (c) duty of care

31

NATURE AND FORMATION

True - False

1. T
2. F
3. T
4. T
5. T
6. F
7. F
8. F
9. F
10. T
11. T
12. T

Multiple Choice

1. A
2. D
3. C
4. C
5. C
6. D
7. A
8. B
9. D
10. A
11. B

Short Essay

1. A corporation is created by statutory authorization; it is a legal entity; it may be perpetual; its shareholders are not generally liable for its debts; its stock is freely transferable; its business is managed by a board of directors; its shareholders are not its agents; it may sue and be sued in its own name.

   A partnership, on the other hand, is created by agreement of the partners; it is a legal entity for some, but not all purposes; it is dissolved by the withdrawal of a partner; its partners are subject to unlimited liability for its debts; the interest of a partner is transferable subject to certain conditions; each partner is entitled to participate in the management of the business; each partner is an agent of the partnership; all partners are parties in actions brought by or against the partnership.

2. A de facto corporation may be formed if:
   (a) there exists a general corporation statute
   (b) there is a bona fide attempt to comply with that law in organizing a corporation under that statute
   (c) there is actual exercise of corporate power by conducting a business in the belief that a corporation has been formed

3. A court will pierce the corporate veil where the shareholders have <u>not</u>
   (a) provided an adequate financial basis for the business
   (b) conducted the business on a corporate basis

32

FINANCIAL STRUCTURE

True - False

1.	F	7.	F
2.	F	8.	T
3.	T	9.	F
4.	T	10.	T
5.	T	11.	F
6.	T	12.	T

Multiple Choice

1.	C	7.	D
2.	D	8.	C
3.	A	9.	A
4.	C	10.	B
5.	B	11.	C
6.	B		

Short Essay

1. A shareholder has the right to
   (a) participate in control of the corporation
   (b) participate in the earnings of the corporation
   (c) participate in the residual assets of the corporation upon dissolution

2. Preferred stock is usually issued with a par value because such stock usually has a liquidation preference which, for all practical purposes, acts as a par value. For example, when stock has a par value, only the consideration received for the stock in excess of par value may be allocated to capital surplus. Likewise, when stock has a liquidation preference, only the consideration received for the stock in excess of the amount of liquidation preference may be allocated to capital surplus, and, when a liquidation preference is provided, preferred stock usually has priority over common to the extent of the par value of the stock.

3. A court will grant an injunction where
   (a) demand has been made upon the directors before commencement of the suit
   (b) earnings or surplus are available out of which a dividend may be declared
   (c) the earnings or surplus is in the form of available cash
   (d) the directors have abused their discretion in withholding a dividend

4. The transferor warrants that
   (a) the transfer is effective and rightful
   (b) the security is genuine and has not been materially altered
   (c) he knows of no fact that might impair the validity of the security

33

MANAGEMENT STRUCTURE

True - False

1. F
2. T
3. F
4. F
5. T
6. T
7. F
8. F
9. T
10. T
11. T
12. T

Multiple Choice

1. C
2. A
3. B
4. A
5. C
6. A
7. B
8. D
9. B
10. C
11. B

Short Essay

1. A shareholder may only inspect the books and records of the corporation for a proper purpose. Thus, a shareholder may be denied his right if he attempts to obtain the information for such improper purposes as use by a competitor or sale to a third party.

2. Shareholder approval is required to make certain fundamental changes in the corporation. These changes include:
   (a) Amending the articles of incorporation
   (b) Reducing the stated capital
   (c) Effecting a merger
   (d) Effecting a consolidation
   (e) Selling or leasing all or substantially all of the assets of the corporation other than in the usual and regular course of business
   (f) Effecting a compulsory share exchange

3. The board of directors has general authority to manage the business and affairs of the corporation. This authority invests the board with the power to:
   (a) select and remove officers
   (b) set management compensation
   (c) determine the capital structure
   (d) declare dividends
   (e) amend the bylaws

4. Directors and officers are required to be
   (a) obedient
   (b) reasonably diligent
   (c) completely loyal

5. Directors and officers are required to perform their duties with such care as an ordinarily prudent person in a like position would use under similar circumstances.

34
FUNDAMENTAL CHANGES

True - False

1. T
2. F
3. T
4. T
5. T
6. T
7. F
8. T
9. T
10. T
11. T
12. F

Multiple Choice

1. D
2. D
3. C
4. A
5. D
6. C
7. B
8. A
9. B
10. C
11. D

Short Essay

1. Fundamental changes include:
   (a) charter amendments
   (b) mergers
   (c) consolidations
   (d) dissolution
   (e) sale or lease of all or substantially all of the corporation's assets not in the usual and regular course of business
   (f) compulsory share exchange

2. Under modern statutes, the typical procedure involves:
   (a) adoption of a resolution by the board setting forth the proposed amendment
   (b) approval by a majority vote of the shareholders
   (c) execution and filing of articles of amendment with the secretary of state
   (d) issuance of the certificate of amendment by the secretary of state

3. This may be accomplished by:
   (a) purchase or lease of the assets
   (b) purchase of a controlling stock interest in the other corporation
   (c) merger with the other corporation
   (d) consolidation with the other corporation

4. A dissenting shareholder must:
   (a) file with the corporation a written objection to the proposed corporate action prior to the vote of the shareholders
   (b) refrain from voting in favor of the proposed corporate action either in person or by proxy
   (c) make a written demand upon the corporation on a form provided by that corporation within the time period set by the corporation, which may not be less than thirty days after the corporation mails the form

35

Secured Transactions and Suretyship

True - False

1. T
2. F
3. F
4. F
5. T
6. F
7. F
8. F
9. T
10. T
11. F
12. T
13. F
14. F
15. T

Multiple Choice

1. C
2. D
3. A
4. A
5. B
6. D
7. C
8. C
9. D
10. B
11. C
12. C

Short Essay

1. There are two steps that a lender must execute in order to obtain a perfected security interest in a boat as collateral for a loan. The first is to create a security interest and have it "attach" to the collateral - the boat. Attachment occurs upon (1) the giving of value by the secured party (the lender); (2) the debtor acquiring rights in the boat; and (3) the secured party takes possession of the boat or a security agreement is entered into which is in writing and which contains a description of the collateral and is signed by the debtor.

   The second step is for the secured party to perfect the security interest. In this case, where the collateral is a boat, perfection is most likely to be effected by filing a financing statement, signed by the debtor, in the appropriate offices. However, perfection can also be obtained by possession or by automatic perfection if the lender satisfies the requirements of a PMSI in consumer goods.

2. (a) Transactions involving real estate are not within the scope of Article 9 of the Code, but instead are subject to State law governing security interests in real property.
   (b) A sewing machine would be treated the same as the boat.
   (c) In most states security interest in motor vehicles must be perfected by a notation on the certificate of title rather than by filing a financing statement.
   (d) Shares of stock are classified as "instruments", and with two

(d) Shares of stock are classified as "instruments", and with two exceptions, the only way to perfect a security interest in them is to take possession of them.

3. A purchase money interest in consumer goods is one in which a seller of consumer goods retains an interest in them by way of a security agreement or by which a lender loans funds for the debtor to purchase the goods. A purchase money security interest in consumer goods is perfected automatically and immediately upon attachment without the necessity of filing a financing statement.

36

BANKRUPTCY

True - False

1. F
2. T
3. T
4. F
5. T
6. F
7. T
8. F
9. F
10. F
11. T
12. F
13. F
14. T

Multiple Choice

1. B
2. A
3. D
4. C
5. D
6. B
7. B
8. C
9. D
10. D
11. D
12. A

Short Essay

1. The bankruptcy process commences with the filing of either a voluntary or an involuntary petition. This filing operates as a stay against attempts by both secured and unsecured creditors to begin or continue to recover claims against the debtor, to enforce judgments against the debtor, or to create or enforce liens against property of the debtor. A trustee is then appointed by the court (he is selcted by a vote of the creditors in proceedings under Chapter 7) to collect, liquidate and distribute the debtor's estate.

2. Discharge is the termination of all debts of the debtor for allowed claims. A discharge of a debt voids any judgment obtained at any time with respect to that debt and operates as an injunction against the commencement or continuation of any action to recover that debt.

   An agreement between a debtor and a creditor permitting the creditor to enforce a discharged debt is enforceable to the extent permitted by state law, but only if:
   (a) the agreement was made before the discharge has been granted;
   (b) the debtor has not rescinded the agreement within 30 days after it becomes enforceable;
   (c) the court has informed a debtor who is an individual that he is not required to enter into such an agreement and explains the legal effect of the agreement; and

(d) if the debt is a consumer debt, the court approves the agreement as not imposing an undue hardship upon the debtor and in the debtor's best interest.

3. The trustee in bankruptcy is made an ideal lien creditor. He possesses every right and power conferred by the law of the State upon its most favored creditor who has acquired a lien by legal or equitable proceedings. He need not locate an actual existing lien creditor, for he assumes the rights and powers of a purely hypothetical lien creditor.

4. A trustee in bankruptcy can recover a preferential transfer from the debtor to a creditor if the transfer was made to or for the benefit of a creditor; for or on account of an antecedent debt owed by the debtor before such transfer was made; made while the debtor was insolvent; made on or within 90 days before the date of the filing of the petition; and that enables such creditor to receive more than he would have received under Chapter 7.

5. At least three non-bankruptcy forms of compromise have been developed to provide relief to debtors. The first is a composition which is a contract or agreement between the debtor and his creditors by which the latter receive a pro rata portion of their claims and the debtor in turn is discharged from the balance of the claims. A second is an assignment for the benefit of creditors, which is a voluntary transfer by the debtor of some or all of his property to a trustee who applies the property to pay all of the debtor's debts. Finally, a court of equity can appoint a disinterested person called a receiver to collect and preserve the debtor's assets and income, and then to dispose of them at the direction of the court that appointed him.

37

TRADE REGULATION

True - False

1. F
2. T
3. T
4. F
5. F
6. F
7. T
8. T
9. F
10. F

Multiple Choice

1. D
2. B
3. D
4. B
5. D
6. C
7. B
8. D
9. C
10. A

Short Essay

1. Federal and State antitrust statutes are designed to prevent unreasonable concentration of economic power which would weaken or destroy free and open competition in the marketplace.

2. Economic theory predicts that the goal of every monopolist is to utilize its power to limit production and increase prices. Thus, a monopolistic market will produce fewer goods at a higher price than a competitive market.

3. Monopolization requires
   (a) sufficient monopoly power
   (b) unfair conduct in attaining or using that power

4. An attempt to monopolize requires
   (a) proof of a specific intent to monopolize
   (b) a dangerous probability of achieving monopoly power

38

SECURITIES REGULATION

True - False

1. F
2. T
3. T
4. F
5. F
6. F
7. T
8. F
9. T
10. T
11. T
12. F
13. F
14. T

Multiple Choice

1. C
2. B
3. C
4. D
5. D
6. D
7. A
8. C
9. C
10. C
11. C

Short Essay

1. The primary purpose of Federal securities regulation is to prevent fraudulent practices in the sale of securities and thereby maintain public confidence in the securities markets.

2. A registration statement usually includes:
   (a) a description of the registrant's properties and business
   (b) a description of the significant provisions of the security to be offered for sale, and its relationship to the registrant's other capital securities
   (c) information about the management of the registrant
   (d) financial statements certified by independent public accounts

3. An issuer must:
   (a) make a reasonable inquiry to determine if the purchaser is acquiring the securities for himself or for others
   (b) provide written disclosure prior to the sale to each purchaser that the securities have not been registered and thus cannot be resold without registration or further exemption
   (c) place a legend on the securities certificate stating that the securities have not been registered and that they are restricted securities

4. The profit is calculated by subtracting the lowest purchase price from the highest sale price that occur within six months of each other. No offset is permitted for losses.

39

CONSUMER PROTECTION

True - False

1. F
2. T
3. T
4. F
5. T
6. F
7. T
8. T
9. F
10. F
11. T

Multiple Choice

1. A
2. B
3. A
4. C
5. B
6. D
7. C
8. B
9. D
10. C

Short Essay

1. A warrantor must:
   (a) disclose in clear and understandable language the warranty that is to be offered
   (b) describe the warranty as either "full" or "limited"
   (c) not disclaim implied warranties if a written warranty is given

2. Under a "full" warranty, the warrantor must:
   (a) agree to repair without charge the product to conform with the warranty
   (b) not limit the duration of any implied warranty
   (c) give the consumer the option of a refund or replacement if repair is unsuccessful
   (d) not exclude consequential damages unless conspicuously noted

3. The creditor must disclose:
   (a) the cost of the credit
   (b) when the finance charge is imposed and how it is computed
   (c) what other charges may be imposed
   (d) whether a security interest is retained or acquired by the creditor

4. The creditor must disclose
   (a) the total amount financed
   (b) the cash price
   (c) the number, amount, and due dates of installments
   (d) delinquency charges
   (e) a description of the security, if any

5. The card issuer may collect up to $50 if:
   (a) the card has been accepted
   (b) the issuer has furnished adequate notice of potential liability to the cardholder
   (c) the issuer has provided the cardholder with a statement of the means by which the issuer may be notified of the loss or theft of the card
   (d) the unauthorized use occurs before the card holder has notified the issuer of the loss or theft
   (e) the issuer has provided a method by which the user can be identified as the person authorized to use the card

40

INTRODUCTION TO REAL AND PERSONAL PROPERTY

True - False

1.	T	6.	T
2.	T	7.	T
3.	T	8.	F
4.	F	9.	T
5.	F	10.	F

Multiple Choice

1.	C	6.	B
2.	B	7.	C
3.	D	8.	C
4.	D	9.	B
5.	D	10.	A

Short Essay

1. Real property consists of all interests in land. Personal property, in contrast, is every other thing or interest identified as property. A fixture is an item of personal property that has been attached to realty so that an interest in it arises under real property law. These classifications are significant in that real and personal property rights are governed by different principles of law.

   Tangible property is property that exists in a physical form; all other property is classified as intangible property. Once again, the determination of various property rights can depend on whether property is classified as tangible or intangible.

2. A fixture is an article or piece of personal property that has been attached in some manner to land or a building so that an interest in it arises under real property law. The intent of the parties as expressed in their agreement will control that determination, but in the absence of an agreement, the courts will look to (1) the physical relationship of the item to the land; (2) the intention of the person who attaches the item to the land; (3) the purpose served by the item in relation to the person who brought it there; and (4) the interest of that person in the land at the time of the attachment of the item.

3. A gift is a transfer of property from one person to another without consideration. A sale, on the other hand, is a transfer of title to specified existing goods for a consideration. The basic defference then, is the lack of consideration needed for an effective gift; in its place, however, is substituted a requirement of completed delivery of the gift.

41

BAILMENTS AND DOCUMENTS OF TITLE

True - False

1. F
2. T
3. T
4. F
5. T
6. T
7. T
8. F
9. T
10. F
11. T

Multile Choice

1. C
2. B
3. D
4. D
5. B
6. D
7. A
8. B
9. D
10. C

Short Essay

1. The four essential elements of a bailment are (1) the delivery of lawful possession of (2) specific personal property by the bailor to the bailee (3) without transfer of title for a determinable time (4) at the end of which the bailee is obligated to return the property either to the bailor or to a person having a superior right of possession.

2. The three kinds of bailments are those for the benefit of the bailee, those for the benefit of the bailor, and mutual benefit bailments. In a mutual benefit bailment, the bailee must exercise the degree of care that a reasonably prudent person would exercise under the same circumstances. If the bailment is one for the benefit of the bailee only, a higher degree of care is expected, and if for the bailor's benefit only, a lower degree of care.

3. Since it is often difficult to show that a bailee's lack of care was the cause of the injury to the bailed goods, the bailor is afforded a presumption that the bailee was at fault. The bailor only needs to show that the goods were delivered by way of bailment and that the bailee failed to return them or that they were returned in a damaged condition. The burden then rests upon the bailee to prove that he exercised the degree of care required of him.

4. Common carriers and private carriers are both bailees, but the common law imposes an extraordinary liability upon the common carrier because of the public nature of its services.

For example, a common carrier has a duty to serve the public to the limits of its capacity and, within those limits, to accept for carriage goods of the kind that it normally transports. A private carrier, however, has no duty to accept goods for carriage except where it agrees to do so by contract.

A private carrier generally is held liable as an ordinary bailee with respect to the goods that it undertakes to carry. The common carrier, on the other hand, is held to a stricter duty that approaches that of an insurer of the safety of the goods.

Finally, both common and private carriers are under an absolute duty to deliver the goods to the person to whom they are consigned by the shipper.

42

INTERESTS IN REAL PROPERTY

True - False

1. T
2 T
3. F
4. F
5. T
6. F
7. F
8. T
9. T
10. T
11. F
12. F

Multiple Choice

1. C
2. C
3. B
4. D
5. D
6. C
7. D
8. C
9. C
10. B

Short Essay

1. The two basic characteristics of the fee simple estate are the holder's absolute rights of transferability and of transmitting by inheritance. In contrast, a qualified fee is one that it is possible to convey or will to another to enjoy absolutely, subject, however, to the possibility that it will be taken away at a later date if a certain event takes place.

2. A reversion is the general interest that the grantor retains if he conveys away less than his entire estate. It is a present estate to be enjoyed in the future. A possibility of reverter exists when the property conveyed may return to the grantor or his successor in interest because of the happening of an event upon which a fee simple estate was to terminate. A possibility of reverter is just an expectancy and is not a present estate. Finally, a remainder is an estate in property that, like a reversion, will take effect in possession if at all upon the termination of a prior estate created by the same instrument. Unlike a reversion, however, a remainder is held by a person other than the grantor or his successors. There are two kinds of remainders - vested and contingent.

3. Under an assignment, both the assignee and the assignor are bound to the obligation to the landlord, as well as with respect to any violations of other covenants that run with the land. A sublease, however, differs from an assignment in that it involves the transfer of less than all of the original tenant's rights in the lease. Moreover, a sublesee's obligations run solely to the original tenant who in turn remains liable to the lessor, and the lessor has no right of action against the sublessee under any of the covenants contained in the original lease. The original tenant, however, remains liable to the landlord in all respects.

4. At common law, a tenant has an implied obligation to pay a reasonable rent at the end of the term. Moreover, a landlord could not remove a tenant for non-payment of rent, but most jurisdictions today have changed that rule by statute. The tenant at common law is not relieved of his liability for rent nor is he allowed to terminate the lease if the premises are destroyed.

   Similarly, the landlord had few implied duties or rights under the common law of leaseholds. He must give the tenant a right to possession at the beginning of the lease, but in most States he is not required to give the tenant actual possession. Moreover, he has an implied duty to provide for the tenant's right to "quiet enjoyment" of the premises. He is, however under no obligation to maintain the premises in a tenantable condition or to make them fit for any purpose, although some courts have abandoned this rule as it applies to residential leases. Finally, except for the common areas remaining under his control, the landlord has no duty to repair the premises.

5. The two types of easements are the easement appurtenant and the easement in gross. The former is more common and the rights created by it pertain to the land itself and not to the particular individuals that created them. Moreover, both the burden and the benefit of an appurtenant easement pass with the land.

   An easement in gross, however, is personal to the particular individual that received the right. It does not depend upon the ownership of the land, and therefore amounts to little more than an irrevocable personal right to use the land.

   A profit a prendre is a right to remove the produce of another's land. Like an easement, a profit may arise by prescription, but if the act of the parties, it must be created with all of the formalities of a grant of an estate in real property. Finally, unless clearly designated as exclusive, a profit is always subject to a similar use by the owner of the land.

   Finally, a license is merely permission to make use of one's land. It creates no interest in the property and is terminable at the will of the grantor. Finally, no formality is necessary to create or to destroy one.

43

TRANSFER AND CONTROL OF REAL PROPERTY

True - False

1. F
2. T
3. T
4. F
5. F
6. F
7. T
8. F
9. T
10. F
11. T

Multiple Choice

1. B
2. D
3. A
4. B
5. C
6. D
7. A
8. B
9. D
10. D
11. D

Short Essay

1. The two essential documents involved in the transfer of real estate are the contract of sale and the deed.

   The contract of sale must be in writing to satisfy the Statute of Frauds. Moreover, it should contain the names and addresses of the parties, a description of the property to be conveyed, the time for the conveyance, the type of deed to be given, and the price and manner of payment.

   A deed must contain a description of the property that is sufficiently clear and certain to permit identification of the property conveyed. It will also usually describe the quantity of the estate conveyed. It will also contain the appropriate covenants of title, if any. Finally, it must be signed by the grantor, and for purposes of recordation, it must be acknowledged before a notary public.

2. The three types of deeds are the warranty deed, the special warranty deed, and the quitclaim deed. By the warranty deed, the seller promises that he has title to the property and that he will do what is necessary to make the grantee whole if the latter suffers any damage because the grantor's title was defective. A warranty deed also conveys after-acquired title.

   In contrast, a special warranty deed is one that warrants only that the title has not been impaired, encumbered or rendered defective by any act or omission of the grantor. The grantor does not warrant that the title may not be defective by reason of the acts of omissions of others.

Finally, a quitclaim deed is used to convey all of one's interest in certain property, whatever it might be. No warranties of title are made.

3. A deed is not effective until it is delivered. "Delivery" means an intent that the deed will take effect and is evidenced by the acts or statements of the grantor. Manual or physical transfer of the deed is usually the best evidence of this intent, but it is not necessary to effect delivery. The deed may be given to a third party escrow agent or even retained in the possession of the grantor. It is treated as delivered when the grantor intends it to be delivered, provided he acts accordingly.

4. A restrictive covenant is a limitation upon the use of one's land - in essence, a negative easement. The restriction is enforceable against all landowners by all landowners in a subdivided common plat to which the restriction applies provided it appears that the restriction was intended to benefit the purchaser of any lot in the tract, and that the restriction appears somewhere in the chain of title to which the lot is subject.

   There are basically two ways that a restrictive covenant can be terminated. First, if it can be shown that there has been a long acquiescence by neighbors in numerous violations of the covenant in the past. Second, the covenant can be terminated if it can be shown that the circumstances that gave rise to the covenant no longer exist.

44
TRUSTS AND WILLS

True - False

1. T
2. F
3. F
4. T
5. F
6. T
7. F
8. T
9. T
10. F
11. T
12. T
13. T

Multiple Choice

1. B
2. B
3. C
4. C
5. C
6. D
7. D
8. C
9. C
10. D

Short Essay

1. The four essential elements of a trust are as follows. First, the trust must have a creator, known as the settlor. Second, there must be a subject matter of the trust, or the trust "corpus" or "res", that is definite and certain. Third, there must be a trustee, but the trust will not fail for want of a trustee because the court will appoint one. Finally, there must be a beneficiary of the trust.

2. A constructive trust is one imposed upon a party to remedy the abuse of a confidential relationship. The property is held in trust by the abusing party for the benefit of the aggrieved party.

   A resulting trust, however, serves to carry out the true intent of the parties in those cases where the intent was inadequately expressed. Both constructive and resulting trusts are created by implication and operation of law and therefore neither has to be in writing.

3. A trust need not be created by particular words provided that the intent of the settlor to establish a trust is unmistakable. Moreover, consideration is not required.

   A trust may be terminated in one of several ways. First, a designated time period may expire or the designated purpose of the trust may end. A trust is irrevocable by the settlor, however, unless he specifically reserves the right, and the trust will not terminate on the death of the trustee or the beneficiary unless their lives are used to measure the duration of the trust.

4. In order to have a valid will, the testator must have both the power and the mental capacity to do so. Moreover, the will must be in writing, signed by the testator, and attested by the State required number (generally two or three) disinterested witnesses. But even if all these requirements are satisfied, a will is revocable by the testator and does not become effective until his death.

5. The first step involved in administering an estate is to see if the deceased left a will. If so, the named executor will handle the administration. If there is no will, the court will appoint an administrator. If there is a will, it is submitted to probate by the personal representative, who then must file an inventory of the estate. Assets are then collected, debts paid, and the remainder disbursed according to either the term of the will, or if there is no will, the laws of intestate succession.

45

INSURANCE

True - False

1. T
2. F
3. T
4. T
5. F
6. F
7. F
8. T
9. F
10. T
11. F
12. T

Multiple Choice

1. B
2. B
3. B
4. D
5. C
6. D
7. B
8. C
9. D
10. D

Short Essay

1. Ordinary life insurance is insurance that accumulates a cash surrender value over time as premiums are paid, but then pays the face value of the policy to the designated beneficiary upon the death of the insured. Term life insurance, however, is issued for a limited number of years. It too will pay proceeds to the designated beneficiary if the insured dies within the specified time period, but it does not accumulate a cash surrender value.

2. Life insurance contracts pay out the face value of the policy to the designated beneficiary upon the death of the insured. An endowment contract contains many similar provisions, but agrees to pay a lump sum of money to the insured when he reaches a certain age or to a beneficiary in the event of the insured's premature death. Finally, an annuity contract is an agreement by the insurer to pay fixed sums at periodic intervals to the insured after he reaches a certain age.

3. An insurable interest is a relationship that a person has to another person, or to certain property such that the happening of a possible specific damage causing contingency would result in direct loss or injury to him. The purpose of the concept is to ensure that insurance is used as protection against the risk of loss resulting from the happening of an event, not the realization of profit from idle wagering.

4. Warranties operate as conditions that must exist before the contract of insurance is effective or before the insured's obligatin to pay is enforceable. Failure of a certain condition to exist or to occur relieves

the insurer from any obligation to perform its promise.

5. Waiver is the intentional relinquishment of a known right; estoppel, on the other hand, means that a person is precluded by his own conduct from asserting a position that is inconsistent with his acts and which have been justifiably relied upon by another.

†